OCR **Psychology**
AS Revision Guide

Cara Flanagan

Psychology Press
Taylor & Francis Group
LONDON AND NEW YORK

First published 2014
by Psychology Press
27 Church Road, Hove, East Sussex BN3 2FA

and by Psychology Press
711 Third Avenue, New York, NY 10017

Psychology Press is an imprint of the Taylor & Francis Group, an informa business

British Library Cataloguing in Publication Data
A catalogue record for this book is available from the British Library

ISBN: 978-1-84872-180-7 (pbk)
ISBN: 978-0-203-79666-5 (ebk)

Typeset in Franklin Gothic
by GreenGate Publishing Services, Tonbridge, Kent

Illustration credits

p. 20: © Lane V. Erickson/Shutterstock.com; p. 24: © Mi.Ti./Shutterstock.com; p. 28: Copyright © 2007 Great Ape Trust; p. 42: © microcosmos/Shutterstock.com; p. 60: © Marta Tobolova/Shutterstock.com; p. 61: From Reicher & Haslam (2006) © The British Psychological Society, published by Wiley; p. 64: From Piliavin *et al.* (1969) © 1969 The American Psychological Association. Reproduced with permission; p. 68: © ollyy/Shutterstock.com; p. 72: © John Springer Collection/CORBIS; p. 76: © Kluke/Shutterstock.com.

Printed and bound in Great Britain by
TJ International Ltd, Padstow, Cornwall

CONTENTS

Unit G541 PSYCHOLOGICAL INVESTIGATIONS

		Tick when you have:	
Pages		Read the text	Completed the activities
2–3	Specification details and information about how Unit G541 is marked		
4	Ethics		
5	Sampling		
6–7	Representing data		
8–9	Observation + exam practice		
10–11	Self-report + exam practice		
12–13	Experiments + exam practice		
14–15	Correlation + exam practice		

Unit G542 THE CORE STUDIES

		Tick when you have:	
Pages		Read the text	Completed the activities
16–17	Specification details and information about how Unit G542 is marked		
18	Methods and issues		
19	Approaches and perspectives		
20–23	Loftus and Palmer (eyewitness testimony)		
24–27	Baron-Cohen et al. (autism)		
28–31	Savage-Rumbaugh et al. (language acquisition)		
32–35	Samuel and Bryant (conservation)		
36–39	Bandura et al. (aggression)		
40–43	Freud (Little Hans)		
44–47	Maguire et al. (taxi drivers)		
48–51	Dement and Kleitman (sleep and dreaming)		
52–55	Sperry (split-brain)		
56–59	Milgram (obedience)		
60–63	Reicher and Haslam (BBC prison study)		
64–67	Piliavin et al. (subway Samaritan)		
68–71	Rosenhan (sane in insane places)		
72–75	Thigpen and Cleckley (multiple personality disorder)		
76–79	Griffiths (gambling)		
81–86	Glossary plus index		

NOTE

This is a revision guide. The information is organised in a way that should aid revision and does contain almost all you need to know.

However, there isn't room to spell out all of the details required for full mark answers to exam questions. This means you sometimes need to consult the main book (*OCR Psychology: AS Core Studies and Psychological Investigations*) for extra detail.

The G541 specification		Tick here when you can do it!
Describe the four techniques	For self-report this should include a knowledge and understanding of rating scales and open and closed questions and the strengths and weaknesses of each.	
	For experiment this should include a knowledge and understanding of experimental design (independent measures and repeated measures) and the strengths and weaknesses of each.	
	For observation this should include a knowledge and understanding of participant and structured observation, time sampling and event sampling and the strengths and weaknesses of each.	
	For correlation this should include a knowledge and understanding of positive and negative correlations and the interpretation of scattergraphs.	
Identify strengths and weaknesses of the four techniques, both in general terms and in relation to source material.		
Frame hypotheses (null and alternate, one- and two-tailed).		
Identify variables (for experiment – identify and explain the difference between independent and dependent variables).		
Suggest how variables might be operationalised/measured.		
Suggest (in relation to source material) strengths and weaknesses of measurement and alternative forms of measurement.		
Comment on the reliability and validity of measurement.		
Describe opportunity sampling, random sampling and self-selected sampling techniques.		
Identify strengths and weaknesses of opportunity, random and self-selected sampling techniques.		
Identify strengths and weaknesses of sampling techniques described in source material.		
Suggest appropriate samples/sampling techniques in relation to source material.		
Suggest appropriate procedures in relation to source material.		
Identify and describe the differences between qualitative and quantitative data.		
Identify strengths and weaknesses of qualitative and quantitative data.		
Suggest appropriate descriptive statistics for data in source material (mean, median, mode).		
Sketch appropriate summary tables/graphs from data in source material (bar charts, scattergraphs).		
Draw conclusions from data/graphs.		
Describe ethical issues relating to psychological research with human participants.		
Identify ethical issues in source material and suggest ways of dealing with ethical issues.		

The G541 exam

1 hour

Total 60 marks

30% of total AS mark

All questions are compulsory

The paper is divided into three sections: sections A, B and C. Each section is worth 20 marks.

The questions will refer to the following four techniques for collecting/analysing data: self-report, experiment, observation or correlation.

In each section of the exam there will be a piece of source material. The source material will be one of the three types explained below:

1. Brief outline of a piece of research

Candidates could be asked to:

- Identify strengths and weaknesses of the research method in general.
- Identify strengths and weaknesses of the specific research described in the source material.
- Suggest improvements to the research and their likely effects.
- Consider issues such as reliability and validity of measurements.
- Consider ethical issues raised by the source material.

2. Data produced by a piece of a research

Candidates could be asked to:

- Suggest appropriate descriptive statistics/graphical representations of data (Note: no inferential statistics are required for this unit).
- Draw conclusions from data/graphs.
- Sketch summary tables/graphs.

3. Outline of a proposed piece of research

Candidates could be asked to:

- Suggest appropriate hypotheses (null/alternate, one-tailed/two-tailed).
- Suggest how variables might be operationalised/measured.
- Suggest appropriate samples/sampling methods.
- Outline possible procedures.
- Evaluate the suggestions they have made.

Exam advice: 2 MARK QUESTIONS

You can see from the mark schemes on the right that two criteria are important:

1 **Clarity** … is about understandability and detail. For example:

   A positive correlation is when two co-variables are increasing.

   This answer would only receive 1 mark because it is not clear what 'are increasing' means.

2 **Context** … is not always required – but when you see the phrase 'in this study', you know you need to include context i.e. reference to the source material. For example:

   One strength of an opportunity sample is that it is easy to do because you just use those people most available.

   This answer would only receive 1 mark because it is a general answer that could be used in relation to any study.

Question: Explain what is meant by a positive correlation. [2]

0 marks	No or irrelevant answer.
1 mark	Attempt to explain what a positive correlation is, but could be **clearer**.
2 marks	**Clear** explanation.

*Question: Describe **one** strength of using an opportunity sample in this study. [2]*

0 marks	No or irrelevant answer.
1 mark	Attempt to suggest a strength but **lacks some clarity** OR strength clearly outlined but **not in context**.
2 marks	Appropriate strength clearly outlined in **context**.

Exam advice: 3 MARK QUESTIONS

Sometimes questions are worth 3 marks. **DETAIL (CLARITY)** and **CONTEXT** are important. For example:

1 mark answer: … One strength of time sampling is you don't have to note down every single behaviour that happens.

2 mark answer: … You don't have to note down every single behaviour that happens. For example you would just look at one boy every 30 seconds.

3 mark answer: … You don't have to note down every single behaviour that happens. For example you would just look at one boy every 30 seconds and note down what he is doing then rather than watching the boy while he is playing and record every target behaviour you see.

To receive 2 marks some context related to the source material must be included.

OR you could add extra DETAIL, for example …you don't have to note down every single behaviour that happens so you will not have to concentrate as hard as you would with event sampling.

To receive 3 marks there is both CONTEXT and DETAIL.

Question: Researchers want to conduct an observation investigating the differences in the way young boys and girls play.

*Give **one** strength of using time sampling in your chosen study. [3]*

0 marks	No or irrelevant answer.
1 mark	Peripherally relevant strength identified, not linked to chosen study (**no contextualisation**) and with little or **no elaboration**.
2 marks	Appropriate strength identified but is basic and **lacks detail**. A vague/weak link is made to the study (**weak contextualisation**) showing **some understanding**.
3 marks	An appropriate strength is **accurately** explained and **elaborated**. There is a clear, developed link to the study (**contextualisation**) showing **good understanding**.

You need these marks because they are critical in determining whether you get a high or low grade. The difference between each grade (e.g. a Grade A and B, B and C, etc.) is usually about 4 marks. If you do badly on a big mark question that alone may cost you two grades.

Exam advice: BIG MARK QUESTIONS

As the title suggests there are some exam questions worth a lot of marks:

Describe an appropriate procedure that could be used in this study. **[10]**

To describe an appropriate procedure you must provide enough detail for **replication**, i.e. enough information for someone else to be able to repeat your procedure. This means you need to be very specific in what you write. Try to include what, who, where and how, as well as materials that might be used.

Gaining a good mark is not about writing lots; examiners say that simple answers are often best as long as the specific details are included.

Describe and evaluate an appropriate procedure that could be used in this study. **[10]**

When evaluation is included this means providing strengths and weaknesses of the procedure you described. As part of a 10 mark question your evaluation should include two or more **APPROPRIATE** evaluation issues in **CONTEXT**.

Evaluate the reliability and validity of this research. **[10]**

One way to approach such questions is to write 'One reason the reliability in this study is good is because …'

To achieve high marks you should clearly separate material on reliability and validity, and should aim to write about four issues (two on reliability and two on validity).

Do not include procedural details when answering such a question – a mistake students often make.

Ethical issues

Informed consent

- Participants are given comprehensive information concerning the nature and purpose of a study and their role in it.
- This is necessary in order that they can make an informed decision about whether to participate.
- From the researcher's point of view this may reduce the meaningfulness of the research because such information will reveal the study's aims and affect participants' behaviour.
- Certain participants are unable to give informed consent (e.g. young children). Parents or guardians are asked instead.

Deception

- This occurs when a participant is not told the true aims of a study (e.g. what participation will involve).
- Thus participants cannot give truly informed consent.
- From the researcher's point of view it might be argued that some deception is relatively harmless and/or can be compensated for by adequate debriefing.

Right to withdraw

- Participants should have the right to withdraw from participating in a study if they are uncomfortable in any way.
- They should also have the right to refuse permission for the researcher to use any data they produce.
- From the researcher's point of view the loss of participants may bias the study's findings.

Protection from harm

- During a research study, participants should not experience negative physical effects, such as physical injury.
- Nor experience psychological effects, such as lowered self-esteem or embarrassment.
- From the researcher's point of view it may not be possible to estimate harm before conducting a study – however any study should be stopped as soon as harm is apparent.
- This can be dealt with using role play.

Privacy

- A person's right to control the flow of information about themselves.
- From the researcher's point of view this may be difficult, for example in a covert observation. Often observers do not wish to alert participants to the fact that they are being studied because that is likely to affect the participant's behaviour.
- Can deal with this by protecting confidentiality and ensuring that all observation is conducted in a public place. However, there isn't universal agreement on what constitutes a public place.

Anonymity and confidentiality

- A participant's right to have personal information protected through anonymity or keeping information safe (confidential).
- The Data Protection Act makes confidentiality a legal right.
- From the researcher's point of view it may not be possible to keep information anonymous/confidential because some details of the study lead to individual's identification.

Exam practice

Study A: Researchers tested the intelligence of school pupils.

Study B: Researchers observed lovers in a public park.

Study C: Researchers interviewed teenage girls with eating disorders about dieting.

In each of the studies above, describe **one** ethical issue that the researchers need to consider when conducting this study and suggest how this could be dealt with. **[4]**

More ways of dealing with ethical issues

Debriefing

- A post-research interview designed to inform participants about the true nature of a study.
- And to restore them to the state they were in at the start of the study.

Ethical guidelines

- Concrete, quasi-legal documents that help to guide conduct within psychology.
- They establish principles for standard practice and competence.
- Published by professional organisations, such as the Code of Conduct produced by the BPS (British Psychological Society).

Ethics committee (also called an institutional review board IRB)

- A group of people within a research institution that must approve a study before it begins.
- May consist of both professional and lay people.
- Considers how the researcher proposes to deal with any ethical issues that arise.
- Weighs up cost-benefit issues.

Presumptive consent

- A method of dealing with lack of informed consent or deception.
- Asking a group of people who are similar to the participants whether they would agree to take part in a study.
- If this group of people consent to the procedure in the proposed study, it is presumed that the real participants would agree as well.

Sampling techniques

Opportunity sample A sample of participants produced by selecting people who are most easily available at the time of the study.

How? e.g. ask people walking by you in the street, i.e. select those who `are available.	
(+) Easiest method because you just use the first participants you can find, which means it takes less time to locate your sample than if using one of the other techniques.	(−) Inevitably biased because the sample is drawn from a small part of the **target population**.

Self-selected sample A sample of participants produced by asking for volunteers.

How? e.g. advertise in a newspaper or on a noticeboard.	
(+) Access to a variety of participants (e.g. all the people who read a newspaper) which may make the sample more representative and less biased. (+) A convenient way to find willing participants. Researchers need committed participants for time-consuming studies.	(−) Sample is biased because participants are likely to be more highly motivated and/or with extra time on their hands (= **volunteer bias**).

Random sample A sample of participants produced by using a **random technique** such that every member of the target population has an equal chance of being selected.

How? Using a random technique, e.g. placing all names in a hat and drawing out the required number.	
(+) Unbiased, all members of the target population have an equal chance of selection. Although you may end up with a biased sample because not all of the participants who are identified will agree to participate.	(−) Takes more time and effort than other methods because you need to obtain a list of all the members of your target population, then identify the sample and then contact the people identified and ask if they will take part.

See
www.psypress.com/books/
details/9781848721807/
for suggested answers.

Some relevant terms

Attrition
* The loss of participants from a study over time.
* This is likely to leave a biased sample or a sample that is too small.

Sampling
* The process of taking a **sample**.
* The process of sampling aims to produce a representative selection of the target population.

Random technique
* Method of selection that ensures each member of the population has an equal chance of being selected.
* For example placing all names in a hat and drawing out the required number.
* Or assigning each person a number and using a random number table.

Target population
* The group of people that the researcher is interested in.
* The group of people from whom a sample is drawn.
* The group of people about whom generalisations can be made.

Volunteer bias
* A form of sampling bias.
* Occurs because volunteer participants are usually more highly motivated than randomly selected participants.

Quantitative and qualitative data

Quantitative data	(+) Easier to analyse because data is in numbers which can be summarised using **descriptive statistics** (averages as well as simple graphs). (+) This generally makes it easier to draw conclusions because, for example, you can see at a glance that men did better on a particular maths test than women, or that the average rating for a particular film was 7 out of 10.	(–) Oversimplifies reality and human experience because it suggests that there are simple answers (statistically **significant** but humanly insignificant).
Qualitative data	(+) Represents the true complexities of human behaviour because access is gained to thoughts and feelings that may not be assessed using quantitative methods. (+) Provides rich details of how people behave because they are given a free range to express themselves.	(–) More difficult to detect patterns and draw conclusions because of the large variety of information collected, and because words cannot be reduced to a few simple points.

Descriptive statistics

Descriptive statistics are used to describe and summarise data.

Tables and graphs

For example **bar charts** and **scattergraphs** (covered on page 14).

Averages

There are three different ways to express the average or typical value of a set of data:

Exam advice

When producing graphs – always ensure they are clearly labelled.

When reporting findings – just state the most obvious, e.g. the most popular or common behaviour and the least common or popular.

Mean	How? Add up all the numbers and divide by the number of numbers. Not appropriate for data in categories.	
	(+) It makes use of the *values* of all the data. Note the use of the word 'values'. All measures of central tendency use all the data and use the data values. But the mean is the only one that uses *all* the values when making the final calculation.	It can be unrepresentative of the numbers if there are extreme values. For example: 2, 4, 5, 6, 9, 10, 12 mean = 6.86 2, 4, 5, 6, 9, 10, 29 mean = 9.42
Median	How? Place all values in order from largest to smallest and select the middle value. If there are two middle values calculate the mean of these two values.	
	(+) Not affected by extreme scores. For example in the data sets above right, the median in both cases would be 6.	(–) Not as 'sensitive' as the mean because not all values are reflected in the median.
Mode	How? Identify the group or groups which is/are most frequent or common.	
	(+) Useful when the data is in categories. For example, asking people to name their favourite colour. The mode would be the colour that received the most votes.	(–) Not a useful way of describing data when there are several modes. For example if 12 people choose yellow and 12 people choose red and 10 people choose purple, the **modal groups** are yellow and red but this isn't very useful information.

Study A

A researcher was investigating sleeping habits in people. The data was going to be used to provide advice to people who have sleep problems in order for them to understand what 'normal' sleep was like. The researcher planned to collect both quantitative and qualitative data.

1   (a)   What is quantitative data? **[2]**
     (b)   Suggest **one** quantitative piece of data that might be collected in this study. **[2]**
     (c)   Outline **one** strength and **one** weakness of quantitative data in this study. **[4]**
2   (a)   What is qualitative data? **[2]**
     (b)   Suggest **one** qualitative piece of data that might be collected in this study. **[2]**
     (c)   Outline **one** strength and **one** weakness of qualitative data in this study. **[4]**

Exam focus on 2 mark questions

For 2 marks, remember that you need to add clarity or context for that important extra mark.

The phrase 'in this study' means you should place your answer in the context of the study.

Study B

Researchers conducted a study into friendships on Facebook. They calculated the mean number of friends that boys and girls had, and found that girls had more friends than boys.

1   (a)   Explain what is meant by the descriptive statistic called the 'mean'. **[2]**
     (b)   Explain how the mean would have been calculated for the males and females in this study. **[4]**
     (c)   Why would the descriptive statistic called the mean be more appropriate than the median? **[2]**

Study C

A psychologist recorded student behaviour when studying in a library. The table below shows the observations of one student made over a period of one hour. Observations were made once a minute and behaviour recorded.

Making notes	Reading	Gazing into space	Talking	Packing/unpacking bag
15	12	5	4	2

1   (a)   Sketch an appropriate graph or chart to display the findings from this study. **[4]**
     (b)   Outline **two** findings from the data displayed in this graph or chart. **[4]**
2   (a)   What behaviour is the mode and how do you know this? **[2]**
     (b)   Outline **one** strength for using the mode in this study. **[2]**

Exam focus on 3 mark questions

'Evaluation' questions ask for a strength or a weakness. Sometimes these questions are worth 2 marks each, and sometimes they are worth 3 marks.

When evaluation questions are worth 3 marks you must make sure you have provided both clarity and context for the full 3 marks.

Clarity and context are explained on page 3.

Study D

Psychologists were asked to evaluate four different treatments used with businessmen who had developed heart conditions. There were 20 people assigned to each treatment group. At the end of the study each businessman's blood pressure was rated on a scale of 1 to 30. The median scores for each group are shown in the graph on the right.

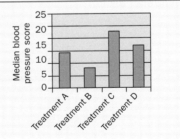

1   Outline **two** findings from the data displayed in this graph or chart. **[4]**
2   (a)   Identify whether the data collected would be quantitative or qualitative. **[1]**
     (b)   Outline **one** strength of using this kind of data in this study. **[3]**
3   (a)   Explain what is meant by the descriptive statistic called the median. **[2]**
     (b)   Explain how the median would have been calculated for each treatment group in this study. **[4]**
     (c)   Why would the descriptive statistic called the 'median' be more appropriate than using the mean? **[2]**

See www.psypress.com/ books/details/ 9781848721807/ for suggested answers.

What people say they do is often different from what they actually do, so observations give a different take on behaviour than other research methods.

Observation

Controlled observation		
Some variables are controlled by the researcher, e.g. in a **laboratory**.	(+) Controlled environment allows focus on particular aspects of behaviour, e.g. playing with certain toys.	(−) Environment may feel unnatural; then participant's behaviour is unnatural (observations lack **validity**).
Naturalistic observation		
Everything is left as normal. Environment unstructured, but may use structured techniques.	(+) A realistic picture of natural, spontaneous behaviour, therefore high **ecological validity**.	(−) Participants may know they are being observed, which alters their behaviour. (−) Little control of other variables.

Observation techniques

Unstructured observation		
Observer records all relevant behaviour but has no system.	(+) Useful when the behaviour to be studied is largely unpredictable. (+) Used in initial investigations as a **pilot study**.	(−) Behaviours recorded often those that are most eye-catching but may not be the most important or relevant behaviours.

Structured observation		
A system is used to restrict and organise the collection of information.	(+) Improves **inter-rater reliability** because observations can be more consistent.	(−) Observer may 'see' what they expect to see (**observer bias**).
Behavioural categories Objective methods to separate continuous stream of action into components, e.g. **behaviour checklist** or **coding system**.	(+) Enables systematic observations to be made so important information is not overlooked.	(−) Categories may not cover all possibilities, some behaviours not recorded (low validity). (−) Poorly designed behaviour checklist also reduces **reliability**.
Sampling **Event sampling** – counting the number of behaviours in a specified time period. **Time sampling** – recording behaviours at regular intervals, or taking a sample at different times of day.	(+) Both methods make the task of observing behaviour more manageable rather than the observer being overwhelmed by every single behaviour. (+) Event sampling is useful when the behaviour to be recorded only happens occasionally. Missing events would reduce validity.	(−) Observer may miss some observations if too many things happen at once, which reduces validity. (−) Observations may not be representative. (−) Time sampling may decrease reliability as it is more difficult to be consistent if recording behaviour during many different time intervals.

Other aspects of observational design

Participant observation Observer is also a participant in the behaviour being observed.	(+) Likely to provide special insights into behaviour from the 'inside'. (+) Able to monitor and record behaviour in closer detail.	(−) Objectivity reduced (**observer bias**). (−) More difficult to record and monitor behaviour unobtrusively if the observer is part of the group being observed.
Disclosed observation Participant is aware of being observed.	(+) Avoids lack of **informed consent** because participants can decide whether to participate.	(−) If participants know they are being observed they are likely to alter their behaviour.
Undisclosed (covert) observation Observations made without a participant's knowledge.	(+) Participants behave more naturally because they are not aware of being observed.	(−) Raises **ethical issues** about observing people without their knowledge (**deception** and invasion of **privacy**).

Evaluating the reliability of observation

Reliability concerns the consistency of observations made, e.g. two observers should be consistent in the record they make (inter-rater reliability). A **correlation** can be used to calculate the association between observations.

Low reliability can be improved by training observers and/or improving behavioural categories.

Evaluating the validity of observation

Validity concerns the 'trueness' of observations. This may be affected by: observer bias, poorly designed behavioural categories (e.g. not everything is recorded), **sampling** procedures (e.g. not enough time to record everything), participant's awareness of being studied.

Study A

A researcher conducts an observation study of people at a stand-up comedy club. The table below shows the observations made by two observers over a 30 minute period using event sampling.

	No expression	Talking to friend	Smiling	Laughing slightly	Laughing loudly
Observer A	6	6	9	12	18
Observer B	4	5	11	15	11

1 (a) Explain what is meant by inter-rater reliability in observational research. [2]
  (b) Explain why the researcher might be concerned about inter-rater reliability in this observation. [4]
  (c) Suggest how the researcher could ensure that this observation has inter-rater reliability. [4]

2 (a) What is event sampling? [2]
  (b) Identify **one** strength and **one** weakness of using event sampling in this study. [4]

3 (a) Sketch an appropriate graph or chart to display the findings from this study. [4]
  (b) Outline **one** finding from this study. [2]

See www.psypress.com/books/ details/9781848721807/ for suggested answers.

Study B

A researcher conducted a study using the participant observation method to investigate people's behaviour while in a dentist's waiting room.

1 (a) What is participant observation? [2]
  (b) Identify **one** strength and **one** weakness of using the participant observation method in this study. [4]

2 Describe and evaluate an appropriate procedure that could be used in this study. [10]

3 Describe **one** ethical issue that the researcher needs to consider when conducting this observation and suggest how this could be dealt with. [4]

Exam focus on 'describe and evaluate an appropriate procedure'

When **DESCRIBING** an observational study you should provide sufficient detail for **replication**:

● **What?** What are the aims of your study?

● **Who?** Who are the target individuals are you going to observe? How many? What are their characteristics?

● **Where?** The geographical location of the observations, and also the position where the observer would be placed.

● **Materials?** The behaviour checklist and the behavioural categories.

● **How?** Must include whether using time or event sampling.

EVALUATION means providing strengths and weaknesses. As part of a 10 mark question your evaluation should include two or more **APPROPRIATE** evaluation issues in **CONTEXT**.

Study C

Some studies observe the behaviour of animals. A researcher decided to turn the tables and observe people at a zoo, when they were watching the animals. The researcher conducted a structured observation of one person at a time as they stood in front of the monkey cages using time sampling.

1 (a) Explain what is meant by 'structured observation'. [2]
  (b) Aside from time sampling, explain **one** other method used to structure observations. [2]

2 (a) What is time sampling? [2]
  (b) Describe **one** strength and **one** weakness of time sampling if it were to be used in this study. [4]
  (c) Explain the difference between time sampling and event sampling in observational research. [4]

3 Outline **one** strength and **one** weakness of conducting observational research in this study. [6]

Study D

Researchers wish to compare the hand gestures used by people from different cultural groups. For example, in some cultures speakers use lots of hand gestures but in others there is limited hand movement when talking. Another difference lies in the signs that are used, for example the thumbs up sign has different meanings in different cultures.

1 (a) Describe an appropriate procedure that could be used in this study. [6]
  (b) Evaluate the reliability and validity of carrying out the study in this way. [6]

2 (a) The data produced in this study is quantitative. What is quantitative data? [2]
  (b) Outline **one** strength and **one** weakness of quantitative data in this study. [4]
  (c) Explain how qualitative data could be collected in this study. [2]

The most obvious way to find out what a person feels, thinks or does is to ask them.

Self-report methods

	Permits a researcher to find out what people think and feel.	Answers may not be truthful (lack **validity**), e.g. because of **leading questions** and **social desirability bias**.
Questionnaire Respondents record their own answers. The questions are predetermined (i.e. structured).	(+) Can be easily repeated so that data can be collected from large numbers of people relatively cheaply and quickly. (+) Respondents may feel more willing to reveal personal/**confidential** information in a questionnaire than in an interview.	(−) The **sample** may be biased because only certain kinds of people fill in questionnaires – literate individuals who are willing to spend time filling them in.
Structured interview Predetermined questions i.e. a questionnaire that is delivered in real-time (e.g. over the telephone or face to face).	(+) Can be easily repeated. (+) Easier to analyse than unstructured interviews because answers are more predictable.	(−) The interviewer's expectations may influence the answers the interviewee gives (this is called **interviewer bias**).
Semi-structured interview New questions are developed as you go along. **Unstructured interview** No questions are decided in advance.	(+) Generally more detailed information can be obtained from each respondent than in a structured interview because the questions are specially shaped to the participant. (+) Can access information that may not be revealed by predetermined questions.	(−) More affected by interviewer bias than structured interviews because the interviewer is developing questions on the spot – they may inadvertently ask leading questions. (−) Requires well-trained interviewers, which makes it more expensive.

Open question Invites respondents to provide their own answers.	(+) Provides rich details of how people behave because they are given a free range to express themselves (provides **qualitative data**). They can express what they actually think rather than being restricted by preconceived categories.	(−) More difficult to detect patterns and draw conclusions because respondents' answers are likely to be different. Therefore a researcher may look for trends rather than using **descriptive statistics**.
Closed question Has limited choices.	(+) Easier to analyse because data is in numbers (**quantitative data**) which can be summarised using averages as well as simple graphs. (+) This generally makes it easier to draw conclusions.	(−) May not permit people to express their precise feelings and tends not to uncover new insights. (−) Oversimplifies reality and human experience because it suggests that there are simple answers.
Rating scale Respondents are asked to give a rating for their answers, e.g. use a scale from 1 to 5 where 5 represents very positive and 1 represents very negative.	(+) A reasonably objective way to represent feelings and attitudes about something, producing quantitative data.	(−) Respondents may avoid ends of scales and go for 'middle of the road', thus answers do not represent true feelings.

Evaluating the reliability of self-report

The **reliability** (consistency) of a person's answers may be affected by:

- The time of day – a person may be less willing to answer fully if questioned later in the day when they are tired.
- Presence of other people – a person may be less willing to answer truthfully if surrounded by other people.
- Ambiguous questions – participants interpret these differently each time they are asked.

Test–retest method can be used to evaluate reliability. The interval between test and retest must be long enough so that the participant can't remember their previous answers but not too long because then their thoughts or feelings may have changed and we would expect their score to be different.

Evaluating the validity of self-report

The **validity** (truthfulness) of a person's answers may be affected by:

- Social desirability bias – participants give answers that make them appear to be 'good'.
- Leading questions – the form of the question 'suggests' what answer is desired.
- **Demand characteristics** – participants respond to other cues from the researcher, participants are trying to help the researcher fulfil the research aims.

Study A

A researcher was interested in testing the effectiveness of a new therapy for treating depression. In order to assess effectiveness, patients were interviewed by a trained therapist about how they were feeling. The interviews were conducted before and after treatment.

1 (a) Explain what is meant by an 'open question' and a 'closed question'. **[4]**
    (b) Outline **one** strength and **one** weakness of using open questions in this study. **[4]**
    (c) Outline **one** strength and **one** weakness of using closed questions in a study investigating how depressed participants felt. **[4]**

2 Describe how a self-selecting sampling technique could be used to obtain participants for this study. **[3]**

3 (a) Identify **one** ethical issue in this study. **[2]**
    (b) Suggest how this ethical issue could be addressed. **[3]**

Study B

A psychologist designed a questionnaire to assess people's phobias (extreme fears) of various animals.

1 (a) Suggest a question that participants could be asked in this study, using a rating scale. **[2]**
    (b) Outline **one** advantage of using a question involving a rating scale in this study. **[2]**

2 (a) Suggest **one** closed question that could be used to investigate people's fears. **[2]**
    (b) Discuss the validity of the closed question you have suggested to investigate people's fears. **[4]**

3 Describe and evaluate an appropriate sampling technique for this study. **[10]**

Study C

A study investigating early childhood memories was conducted by psychologists. They were interested to find out about people's earliest memories using self-report methods.

1 Describe and evaluate an appropriate procedure that could be used in this study. **[10]**

2 (a) What is qualitative data? **[2]**
    (b) Outline **one** strength and **one** weakness of qualitative data in this study. **[4]**

3 Identify **one** strength and **one** weakness of using the self-report method in this study. **[4]**

Exam focus on 'describe and evaluate an appropriate procedure'

The same guidelines apply as given for observational studies – describe what, who, where, materials and how (see page 9).

In the case of a self-report study it would be useful to include some examples of the questions that would be used.

It is important to realise that marks are not awarded for writing lots, nor are they awarded for complex designs. Keep the design simple and make sure you include specific details so that replication would be possible.

See www.psypress.com/books/ details/9781848721807/ for suggested answers.

Study D

A researcher investigated TV viewing habits in younger and old people using the self-report method. Participants were asked closed questions. The participants were selected using opportunity sampling. Some of the findings from this study are displayed in the table below.

	Mean hours watched per week	Kind of programme watched		
		Sport	Comedy	Drama
Older participants (age 40–59)	12	30%	20%	50%
Younger participants (age 20–39)	13	35%	33%	32%

1 Evaluate the reliability and validity of this research. **[10]**

2 Outline **two** findings from the data in this table. **[4]**

3 Name and describe an alternative sampling method for this study. **[2]**

4 (a) Write an open question that could be used in this study. **[2]**
    (b) Evaluate the validity of using this question in this study. **[2]**

Exam focus on 'evaluate the reliability and validity of this research'

On page 3 BIG MARK questions on this topic were discussed. The suggestion was to approach such questions by writing 'One reason the reliability in this study is good is because …'.

Experiments

All experiments have an independent variable (IV) and a dependent variable (DV).

Variables	Hypotheses
Independent variable (IV) is a factor that is directly manipulated by the experimenter in order to observe its effects on the DV. **Dependent variable (DV)** depends in some way on the IV. Variables must be **operationalised**, i.e. defined in a way that they can easily be tested. For example, instead of saying that the DV is 'educational attainment' an experimenter must specify a way to measure this, such as GCSE grades.	An **hypothesis** (also called **alternate hypothesis**) is a precise and testable statement about the relationship between variables such as IV and DV, e.g. *People who smile a lot have more friends than people who don't smile.* **Null hypothesis** is a statement of no difference or no relationship, e.g. *There is no difference in the number of friends of people who smile a lot and those who don't smile a lot.* **One-tailed hypothesis** states the direction of the predicted difference between two conditions or two groups of participants, e.g. *People who smile a lot have more friends than people who do not smile a lot.* **Two-tailed hypothesis** states a difference between two conditions or two groups of participants, without stating the direction of the difference, e.g. *There is a difference in the number of friends of people who smile a lot and those who do not smile a lot.*

Types of experiment

Laboratory experiment A laboratory is a special environment where causal relationships can be investigated under controlled conditions.	(+) Well-controlled. (+) **Extraneous variables** are minimised (increasing **validity**). (+) Can be easily **replicated** because most aspects of the environment have been controlled (enhancing validity and demonstrating **reliability**).	(−) Artificial, a contrived situation where participants may not behave naturally (as they would in day-to-day life). Low **ecological validity**. (−) **Demand characteristics** and **experimenter bias** may reduce validity.
Field experiment An experiment conducted in more everyday surroundings than a laboratory.	(+) Less artificial, and usually higher ecological validity. (+) Avoids demand characteristics and experimenter bias if participants not aware of being studied (increases validity).	(−) Less control of extraneous variables (reduces validity). (−) More time consuming and thus more expensive.
Quasi-experiment Experimenter does not manipulate the IV but uses an IV that would vary even if the experimenter wasn't around.	(+) Allows research where an IV can't be manipulated for **ethical** or practical reasons. (+) Enables psychologists to study 'real' problems, e.g. effects of a disaster on health (increases ecological validity).	(−) Cannot demonstrate causal relationships because IV is not directly manipulated. (−) Less control of extraneous variables (reduces validity). (−) Participants may be aware of being studied (reduces validity).

Experimental design

Repeated measures Each participant takes part in every condition under test (e.g. **experimental condition** and **control condition**).	(+) Good control for **participant variables**. (+) Fewer participants needed.	(−) **Order effects** from doing one condition first (e.g. boredom, practice). Can control with **counterbalancing**. (−) Participants may guess the purpose of the experiment. (−) DV in condition A may be easier than in condition B (an extraneous variable).
Independent measures Participants are allocated to two (or more) **experimental groups** representing different experimental conditions.	(+) Avoids order effects and participants guessing the purpose of the experiment.	(−) Needs more participants. (−) No control of participant variables. Can be dealt with by using **random allocation** of participants to conditions.

Evaluating the reliability of experiments	Evaluating the validity of experiments
Reliability is related to how the DV is assessed and the consistency of this measurement. Measurement may involve observation, **self-report** (e.g. **rating scale**) or a test.	The **validity** ('trueness') of experiments is related to: • Participant awareness • Extraneous variables • Demand characteristics • Order effects • Experimenter bias • Replication • Realism (ecological validity)

Study A

Researchers conducted a repeated measures experiment to find out whether teachers give female students higher marks than male students just because of their gender. In order to conduct this study they obtained two essays judged to be of the same standard and asked 20 teachers to mark both essays. One essay was said to be by Mary Thomas and the other essay was by Robert Jones. The results are shown in the table on the right.

Mean mark awarded if essay was thought to be written by a girl	63
Mean mark awarded if essay was thought to be written by a boy	57

1 (a) What is a *repeated measures design*? **[2]**

    (b) Outline **one** strength and **one** weakness of using a repeated measures design for this investigation. **[6]**

2 (a) What is the independent variable (IV) in this study and how has it been operationalised? **[2]**

    (b) What is the dependent variable (DV) in this study and how has it been operationalised? **[2]**

3 Identify **two** controls that could have been used in this study and explain why they would have been needed. **[6]**

4 Outline **one** conclusion that could be drawn from the table. **[2]**

Exam focus on identifying controls

You should consider factors that must be kept the same for both conditions i.e. controlled so that the only thing that is different is the changed IV.

Study B

A psychologist investigated the effect of leading questions on people's memories. Some participants were asked if they had headaches frequently (a leading question because the question suggests they had them often) whereas other participants were asked how often they had headaches (not a leading question).

1 (a) Suggest an appropriate alternate hypothesis for this experiment. **[3]**

    (b) Identify whether your hypothesis is one-tailed or two-tailed. **[1]**

2 (a) Identify the experimental design used in this study. **[2]**

    (b) Outline **one** strength and **one** weakness of using this experimental design in this study. **[4]**

3 Evaluate both the reliability and validity of the way the dependent variable (DV) has been measured in this study. **[10]**

Exam focus on 'describe and evaluate an appropriate procedure'

The same guidelines apply as given for observational studies – describe what, who, where, materials and how.

Study C

A researcher becomes interested in the effects of simple rewards on behaviour and wants to investigate whether people talk more if you smile at them. The researcher intends to conduct a field experiment using an independent measures design.

1 Suggest an appropriate null hypothesis for this study. **[4]**

2 Explain the difference between an independent measures design and a repeated measures design. **[4]**

3 Identify the independent variable (IV) and dependent variable (DV) in this study. **[2]**

4 Describe and evaluate a suitable procedure for this experimental study. **[10]**

See www.psypress.com/ books/details/ 9781848721807/ for suggested answers.

Study D

A researcher wants to conduct an experiment to investigate differences between people who are left- and right-handed. One area of interest is creativity. The researcher decides to assess this by asking people to rate their creativity on a scale of 1 to 5 where 1 is lacking creativity and 5 is very creative.

1 Explain why this is an experiment. **[2]**

2 (a) Outline **one** strength and **one** weakness of the way that the dependent variable (DV) has been measured in this study. **[6]**

    (b) Describe and evaluate **one** other way to operationalise the dependent variable (DV) in this study. **[10]**

3 Identify a suitable method of obtaining a sample for this study. **[2]**

Exam focus on 'describe and evaluate one other way to operationalise the dependent variable in this study'

Spend some time thinking about how you could do this, don't just plunge in with the first thing that comes to mind.

Next, describe in quite a bit of detail how you would do this (there up to 6 marks for procedure).

Finally, don't forget there are at least 4 marks for the evaluation.

Correlation

A correlation is a way of measuring the relationship between two co-variables.

(+) Can be used when it would be not be **ethical** or practical to conduct an **experiment**. (+) If the correlation is not strong then you can rule out a causal relationship. You can't demonstrate a causal relationship but if there is no correlation between co-variables then there can't be a causal relationship. (+) If the correlation is strong then further investigation is justified because there may be a causal link.	(–) Cannot show a cause-and-effect relationship. (–) People often misinterpret correlations and assume that a cause and effect have been found whereas this is not possible. (–) There may be **intervening variables** that can explain why the co-variables being studied are linked, e.g. assuming that TV causes aggressiveness just because there is a correlation between amount of TV watched and aggressiveness.

Scattergraphs are used to plot the correlational data. Each dot represents one person.

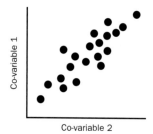

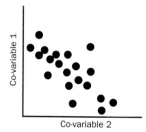

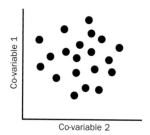

Positive correlation
As one co-variable increases, the other increases.

Negative correlation
As one co-variable increases, the other decreases.

No correlation
No relationship between co-variables.

Writing hypotheses for a correlation study

Null hypothesis (no correlation)	There is no relationship between the co-variables.	For example: *There is no relationship between intelligence and memory.*
Alternate hypothesis	The two co-variables are correlated.	For example: *There is a correlation between intelligence and memory.*

Evaluating the reliability of correlation **Reliability** is related to how the co-variables are measured and assessed and the consistency of this measurement. Measurement may involve observation, **self-report** (e.g. **rating scale**) or a test.	**Evaluating the validity of correlation** The **validity** ('trueness') of correlations is related to the assessment of each co-variable. For example, if one co-variable is memory, we need to consider how this has been assessed and the validity of that assessment.

Study A

A researcher wishes to investigate the effects of poor handwriting on a student's essay marks. In order to do this the researcher conducts a correlation. The researcher expects to find a positive correlation. Fifty student essays are each marked by a teacher and a different person is asked to rate the clarity of the handwriting on a scale of 1 to 10, where 10 is very clear.

See
www.psypress.com/books/
details/9781848721807/
for suggested answers.

1   Explain what is meant by a positive correlation. **[2]**
2   Suggest an appropriate alternate hypothesis for this study. **[4]**
3   (a)   What is quantitative data? **[2]**
    (b)   Suggest **two** examples of quantitative data that could have been collected in this study. **[4]**
4   Describe how data is presented in a scattergraph. **[2]**
5   Evaluate the reliability and validity of carrying out the study in this way. **[6]**

Study B

Researchers conducted a study looking at the relationship between the number of children in a family and their IQ scores. The findings from the study are presented in the scattergraph on the right.

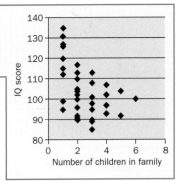

1   (a)   Explain what is meant by a negative correlation. **[2]**
    (b)   Suggest an appropriate null hypothesis for this study. **[4]**
2   (a)   How many participants was data collected from in this study and how do you know this? **[2]**
    (b)   From the scattergraph on the right, what is the mode for the number of children in a family and how do you know this? **[2]**
    (c)   Outline **two** other conclusions from the data in this scattergraph. **[4]**
3   Identify **one** strength and **one** weakness of using the correlation method in this study. **[6]**

Study C

A psychologist investigated whether people who are married are judged as being quite similar in terms of attractiveness. Each partner was rated by an observer in terms of their attractiveness, on a scale of 1 to 10 where 1 is very unattractive and 10 is very attractive. The data collected are shown in the table on the right.

Husband	8	6	4	5	2	8	9	6	7
Wife	6	5	8	6	5	4	8	5	7

1   Sketch an appropriately labelled scattergraph displaying the results of this study. **[4]**
2   (a)   Explain what is meant by a negative correlation. **[2]**
    (b)   Explain why you think this graph does or does not demonstrate a negative correlation. **[2]**
3   Outline **one** strength and **one** weakness of the way 'attractiveness' was measured in the study. **[6]**
4   Describe **one** ethical issue that the researchers need to consider when conducting this correlation and suggest how this could be dealt with. **[4]**
5   Identify **one** strength of the correlational method. **[2]**

Study D

A research planned to investigate the relationship between memory and age.

Exam focus on 'describe and evaluate an appropriate sampling technique for this study'

The 'describe' part must include a detailed explanation of how you would collect the sample. The 'evaluate' part should include strengths and weaknesses.

1   (a)   Outline how memory could be measured in this correlation study. **[4]**
    (b)   Outline **one** strength and **one** weakness of the way you would measure memory in this study. **[6]**
2   Describe and evaluate an appropriate sampling technique for this study. **[10]**

The G542 specification

This unit examines the candidates' knowledge and understanding of the 15 core studies.

It also examines their ability to make evaluative points about the studies and their ability to see the studies in the wider perspective of psychological approaches/perspectives, theories, issues, concepts and methods.

Candidates will be asked questions relating to:

- Specific aspects of the core studies.
- Theories and research surrounding the core studies.
- The approaches/ perspectives, issues and methods arising from the core studies.
- Specific aspects of core studies.
- The background to the studies (the context).
- Theories on which studies are based.
- Psychological perspectives applicable to the studies.
- Other research pertinent to the studies.
- The information in the studies.
- The methods used in the studies.
- The way the results are analysed and presented; the conclusions that can be drawn from the studies.
- Strengths and limitations of the studies.
- The general psychological issues illustrated by the studies.
- Evaluations of all of the above.

The G542 exam

2 hours

Total 120 marks

70% of total AS mark

The paper is divided into three sections:

Section A Core studies

Total 60 marks

All questions are compulsory

For each core study there will be one question worth 4 marks (a total of 15 questions). These questions may be parted. The questions will ask about specific aspects of the core studies.

Section B Core studies, methods and issues

Total 36 marks

There is one question (with six parts) but a choice between three core studies.`

Questions will cover aims, procedures and results of core studies as well as research methods used and issues named in the specification. For example:

Choose one of the following core studies [three studies named] and answer parts (a) – (f) on this study.
(a) *Outline the aim of this study.* **[2]**
(b) *Describe the sample used in this study and suggest **one** advantage of using this sample.* **[6]**
(c) *Outline the procedure of this study.* **[6]**
(d) *Outline the findings of this study.* **[6]**
(e) *Discuss the reliability of the findings of this study.* **[6]**
(f) *Describe and evaluate changes that could be made to the way this study was conducted.* **[10]**

Section C Approaches and perspectives

Total 24 marks

A choice between two questions

Questions take the following form:

(a) *Outline **one** assumption of the XXX approach.* **[2]**
(b) *With reference to named core study, describe how the XXX approach could explain the topic studied.* **[4]**
(c) *Describe **one** similarity and **one** difference between any core studies that take the XXX approach.* **[6]**
(d) *Discuss strengths and weaknesses of the XXX approach using examples from any core studies that take this approach.* **[12]**

Section A advice

*Thorough knowledge of the core studies is essential. You need to know the specific **details**.*

Section B advice

To gain high marks you must:

***Provide detail** The mark schemes on the facing page show that detail is used to assess your answer. Include numbers!*

***Focus** Many students make the mistake of including irrelevant information. For example, when asked about the procedure of a study they include information about the sample or the findings. Irrelevant information gains no marks.*

***Contextualise** Your answer must refer to the core study.*

***Elaborate** You must state your answer and then explain it.*

Section C advice

Detail, focus, contextualisation, elaboration are all important.

In addition, be aware of the following advice:

***Question (a)** The word 'behaviour' must appear in your answer.*

***Question (b)** Must refer back to the assumption in part (a).*

***Question (c)** Use specific examples. You can use one core study for the similarity and a second one for the difference.*

***Question (d)** 'Discuss' means that you first of all must describe the strength/weakness and then must evaluate it, e.g. consider why it is a strength/weakness.*

Two strengths and two weaknesses are sufficient as long as they are well elaborated.

Exam advice: PRODUCING DETAILED ANSWERS

When answering exam questions the number of marks available gives you some guidance about how much you should write – a 2 mark question requires less than a 3 mark question. However, it isn't just about the number of words because one student may write a lot but gain fewer marks than another student because their answer lacks **DETAIL**.

Consider the two examples below, which one would gain more marks?

Student A: *In the study by Baron-Cohen, there were three groups of participants in the sample. The three groups were the children with a kind of autism. There were 16 people in this group. The second group with normal adults, there were 50 in this group. Finally there was a group of 10 people with Tourette syndrome.* (55 words)

Student B: *In the study by Baron-Cohen there were 16 individuals with autism (14 had Asperger syndrome), sex ratio was 13 males : 3 females. All had normal IQ. There was a second control group of normal age-matched adults (equal males to females). The third group of 10 had Tourette syndrome, again age-matched. Sex ratio 8 males : 2 females.* (55 words)

Bearing in mind that detail matters, a rough guide to length is:

- 2 mark answers, about 50 words
- 8 mark answers, about 200 words
- 10 mark answers, about 250 words

Exam advice: CONTEXTUALISATION – THE DROP-IN

Contextualisation applies to many of your examination questions. One way to test whether or not you have contextualised your answer is to imagine taking your answer to one question and dropping it into another question – would it read OK? In which case it has not been contextualised. For example:

*Outline one **weakness** of using independent measures in this study.* [2]

Answer: One weakness of using independent groups design is that you cannot control participant variables so that the participants in one group may be different in some way to the participants in the other group. If the participants in one group were more able that would explain why they did better rather than because of the independent variable.

The problem is that there is nothing in that answer that relates to a specific study. There is no **CONTEXT**. The same answer could be **DROPPED IN** to any question on the weaknesses of independent measures and would not score full marks.

Exam advice: ELABORATION – THE THREE-POINT RULE

S	**State** your point.	**e.g.** One criticism of the study is that it lacks ecological validity.
C	**Context** – provide evidence to support your point.	**e.g.** The study tested memory using a film of a car accident which doesn't reflect how eyewitnesses would actually experience an accident.
C	**Comment** on the significance of your point, or add an explanation, or any further comment.	**e.g.** Lack of ecological validity means you can't generalise the findings to everyday life.

Some examples of mark schemes

6 mark question

For example, *Outline the findings of your chosen study.* [6]

5–6 marks

Outline has **increasing accuracy** and **detail** with several fine details included. Detail is appropriate to level and time allowed. **Understanding, expression** and use of **psychological terminology** is good. There are clear and appropriate links to the study (**clear contextualisation**).

10 mark question

For example, *Describe and evaluate changes that could be made to the way your chosen study was conducted.* [10]

9–10 marks

Description of **two or more changes** is appropriate to the study. Description is **detailed** with **good understanding** and **clear expression**.

Evaluation is effective and well informed. There is a **good balance** between description and evaluation. The answer is competently **structured and organised**. Answer is mostly grammatically correct with occasional spelling errors.

12 mark question

For example, *Discuss the strengths and limitations of the social approach using examples from any core studies that take this approach.* [12]

10–12 marks

There is a **good range** of strengths (2 or more) and weaknesses (2 or more) which are appropriate to the question. There is a **good balance** between the two. **Discussion** is detailed with **good understanding** and clear **expression**. **Analysis** is effective and **argument well informed**. Appropriate use of **supporting examples**. The answer is competently **structured and organised**. Answer is mostly grammatically correct with occasional spelling errors.

G542 Section B questions include questions about methods and issues

The following topics are covered on pages 4–15. Example questions for Section B are shown below and throughout this section of the book.

Sampling	Experimental (laboratory and field)
*Describe how the sample in this study was selected and suggest **one** advantage of using this sample.* **[6]**	*Explain why this study can be considered a laboratory experiment.* **[6]**
	*Give **one** advantage and **one** disadvantage of conducting this study in the field.* **[6]**
Ethics	**Self-report**
*Describe **two** ethical issues raised by this study.* **[6]**	*Describe how self-report was used in this study.* **[6]**
*With reference to this study, explain **one** reason why the researcher(s) needed to break ethical guidelines and **one** reason why they should not have done so.* **[6]**	*Suggest **one** strength and **one** weakness of using self-report in this study.* **[6]**
Suggest how this study could be made more ethical. **[8]**	
Qualitative and quantitative data	**Observation**
Briefly outline how qualitative data was gathered in this study. **[2]**	*Describe how observation was used in this study.* **[6]**
*Describe **two** examples of qualitative data in this study.* **[4]**	*Suggest **one** strength and **one** weakness of using observation in this study.* **[6]**
*Suggest **one** strength and **one** weakness of qualitative data in this study.* **[6]**	

Methodological issues such as reliability and validity and ecological validity
Discuss the reliability of the findings of this core study. **[6]**
Discuss the validity of this study. **[6]**
*Outline **two** ways in which this study can be said to be low in ecological validity.* **[4]**
*Outline **one** way in which the study was high in ecological validity.* **[2]**

The following topics are not included on pages 4–15, therefore extra information has been provided to use in G542. Example questions for Section B are shown below and throughout this section of the book.

Case study	A research investigation that involves a detailed study of a single individual, group of people, institution or event.	
*Give **two** advantages of the case study method as used in this study.* **[6]**	(+) Provides rich, in-depth data, so information that may be overlooked using other research methods may be identified.	(−) It is difficult to generalise from individual cases as each one has unique characteristics.
	(+) Can be used to investigate instances of behaviour that are rare (e.g. mental illness).	(−) It is often necessary to use recollection of past events and such evidence may be unreliable.
	(+) The complex interaction of many factors can be studied.	(−) Researchers may lack objectivity because they get to know the case.

Longitudinal and snapshot	A **longitudinal study** looks at changes in behaviour over a long period of time (it is not simply a study that spans a long period of time).	
Explain why this study can be considered a snapshot study. **[4]**	A **snapshot study** looks at behaviour at one moment in time.	
*With reference to this study, suggest **one** strength and **one** weakness of conducting snapshot studies.* **[6]**	(+) Longitudinal studies control **participant variables**.	(−) Such studies usually take a long time to complete.
	(+) Researchers can compare participants to test the effect of time on an IV (repeated measures).	(−) **Attrition** is a problem because some of the participants inevitably drop out over the course of a study. These are likely to be the less motivated or less happy ones, leaving a biased **sample**.
		(−) Participants are likely to become aware of the research aims.
		(−) **Cohort effects** mean that the group studied may be unique and the results won't be generalisable.
	(+) Snapshot studies are relatively quick.	(−) The two groups of participants may be quite different, therefore results may be due to participant variables rather than the IV.
	(+) Researchers can test effects of time or other IV by using two (or more) groups.	(−) Cohort effects mean that one group may not be comparable to another because they had different experiences.

> For each core study you need to consider how this study illustrates one of the approaches and, in some cases, one of the perspectives as well.

G542 Section C questions relate to the seven approaches and perspectives outlined below

An example question for Section C is shown on the right and there are more throughout this section of the book.

The table below provides information to help answer these questions.

Section C questions

(a) Outline **one** assumption of the XXX approach. **[2]**
(b) With reference to named core study, describe how the XXX approach could explain the topic studied. **[4]**
(c) Describe **one** similarity and **one** difference between any core studies that take the XXX approach. **[6]**
(d) Discuss strengths and weaknesses of the XXX approach using examples from any core studies that take this approach. **[12]**

Cognitive approach

The assumption of the cognitive approach is that internal mental activity can be used to explain behaviour. Mental activities include memory, perception, language, thought, decision-making and so on.

(+) A scientific approach – produces clear predictions that can be tested.
(+) Has had many useful applications.
(+) Tends to produce **quantitative data** which are easier to analyse.

(−) A mechanistic approach, suggesting that human thinking is like a computer.
(−) Ignores some important influences on behaviour, such as social influences.
(−) Research methods have low **ecological validity**.

Developmental approach

The assumption of the developmental approach is that there are clearly identifiable and systematic changes that occur in behaviour as a consequence of age and/or experience.

(+) Recognises that behaviour changes through the lifespan.
(+) Adds to our understanding of the interaction between **nature** and **nurture**.

(−) Often claimed to be **reductionist** because complex behaviours reduced to a single factor (age).
(−) Many proposals about age-related changes are too rigid.

Physiological approach

The assumption of the physiological approach is that behaviour can be explained through processes in the body and the brain.

> The word 'behaviour' must appear in any answer about the assumptions of an approach.

(+) A scientific approach – measurable variables enable well-controlled, objective research.
(+) Provides a strong counter-argument to the nature side of the nature–nurture debate.

(−) A reductionist approach as complex behaviours are reduced to brain activity.
(−) Tends to ignore individual differences.
(−) Research methods have low ecological validity.

Social approach

The assumption of the social approach is that our behaviour is influenced by the people around us and the interactions between us.

(+) Helps in understanding the powerful effects of other people on our behaviour.

(−) Underestimates the influence of individual differences on behaviour.
(+) Overemphasises the influence of social and cultural factors, ignoring factors such as biology.

Individual differences

The assumption of the individual differences approach is that everyone's behaviour is not the same. We should focus on how people differ as well as trying to make generalisations about how people behave.

(+) Allows psychologists to learn more about behaviour because all behaviours are studied, not just average ones.
(+) Focus on what makes people different rather than seeking to make generalisations.

(−) Techniques not fully objective and thus results may be biased.
(−) Raises **ethical issues** in studying people who are labelled as 'different'.

Behaviourist perspective

The assumption of the behaviourist perspective is that all behaviour is learned through direct experience (**classical** and **operant conditioning**) or indirect rewards (**social learning**).

(+) A scientific approach – concepts are easily **operationalised**.
(+) Provides a strong counter-argument to the nurture side of the nature–nurture debate.

(−) Ignores biological and innate explanations.
(−) A **determinist** approach because it suggests people are controlled by environmental factors.
(−) Relies on **laboratory** studies which may lack ecological validity.

Psychodynamic perspective

The assumption of the psychodynamic perspective is that behaviour is driven by unconscious thoughts and feelings, often stemming from childhood experiences.

(+) Combines both nature and nurture – an interactionist approach.
(+) Encourages the collection of **qualitative data** using the **case study** method.

(−) A determinist approach because it suggests people are controlled by their unconscious.
(−) Not a scientific approach – concepts are difficult to test.
(−) Methods may lack objectivity.

Loftus and Palmer

Aim

The aim of the first experiment is to investigate the accuracy of memory and, in particular, the effect of leading questions on what people remember.

The aim of the second experiment is to see if the leading question changed a person's subsequent memory of the event they witnessed.

Context

Research into memory

Psychologists have shown that our memories do not simply record what happens. Our memories are not accurate; in fact they can be very inaccurate.

Leading questions

Certain questions or statements are phrased in a way that leads a person to give a particular answer. They are more 'suggestive' than others. In legal terms such questions are called **leading questions** – a question that '*either by its form or content, suggests to the witness what answer is desired or leads him to the desired answer*' (Loftus and Palmer, 1974, page 585).

Estimating speed

Psychological research has found that people are very inaccurate when asked to estimate the speed of a vehicle. For example, Marshall (1969) found that Air Force personnel were very inaccurate. The personnel knew in advance that they would be asked to estimate the speed of a vehicle. When they observed a car travelling at 12 mph, their estimates of the speed ranged from 10 to 50 mph.

This suggests that it might be quite easy to influence the answers that people give to such numerical questions.

Where does it all go wrong?

There are two experiments in this study. Students get confused about what goes with each experiment and why:

Experiment 1
5 groups
Testing whether leading questions distort recall

Experiment 2 Part 1 – similar to experiment 1 Part 2 – broken glass question
3 groups (2 experimental groups, 1 control)
Testing whether leading questions affect storage or retrieval

Procedure

Experiment 1

1 Participants were shown seven film clips of car accidents.
2 They were asked questions about the film clips including one critical question: *How fast were the cars going when they [insert verb] each other?*
3 Participants were given one of five different verb conditions:
   - Group 1: the verb was 'hit'.
   - Group 2: the verb was 'contacted'.
   - Group 3: the verb was 'smashed'.
   - Group 4: the verb was 'bumped'.
   - Group 5: the verb was 'collided'.

Experiment 2

Part 1

4 Participants were shown a film of a car accident.
5 They were again asked questions about the film clips, including the critical question about speed: *How fast were the cars going when they [insert verb] each other?*
   - **Experimental group 1:** The verb was 'smashed'.
   - Experimental group 2: The verb was 'hit'.
   - Group 3 (**control group**): There was no question.

Part 2

6 The participants were asked to return to the laboratory a week later.
7 They were asked some more questions about the film clips they had seen a week earlier. One of the questions was 'Did you see any broken glass?' (There was no broken glass in any of the film clips.)

Sample

- **Experiment 1**: 45 American college students (divided into five groups).
- **Experiment 2**: 150 American college students (divided into three groups).

The article does not state how the participants were selected.

(+) It's easy for college staff to obtain college students as participants.
(−) The participants were American students, therefore not generalisable.

Research method/technique

This is a **laboratory experiment**, using **independent measures**.

Experiment 1 is a **snapshot** study.

IV = Verb used to describe the accident

DV = Estimate of speed

Hypothesis = Participants in each group provide different estimates of the speed the car was travelling at the time of the accident.

Experiment 2 is a **longitudinal** study (studying the effect of passing time).

IV = Verb used to describe the accident

DV = Reporting whether there was broken glass or not

Hypothesis = Participants who believe the car was travelling faster (the 'smashed' group) are more likely to report broken glass than participants in the other two groups ('hit' and control group).

(+) Other variables that influence the estimate of speed can be controlled.
(−) Artificial, contrived situation – in a real life accident, participants care more and may have more accurate memories.

Findings

Experiment 1

- The **mean** speed estimates were faster for those who had the verb 'smashed' (40.8 mph) than those with the verb 'contacted' (31.8 mph).
- The mean speed estimates for the other groups were 'collided' 39.3, 'bumped' 38.1, 'hit' 34.0.
- Participants were not able to accurately estimate speed. In four of the films the accident took place at the following speeds: 20 mph, 30 mph, 30 mph and 40 mph – yet participants' mean estimates for all of these was between 36 and 40 mph.

Experiment 2

- The mean speed estimates were faster for those who had the verb 'smashed' (10.46 mph) than those with the verb 'hit' (8.0 mph).
- More participants who had the verb 'smashed' reported seeing broken glass (16 participants) than other participants.
- In the other groups, seven participants with the verb 'hit' reported broken glass and six participants in the control group reported broken glass.
- Overall, most participants correctly reported seeing no broken glass (121 out of 150).

Quantitative data e.g. the estimates of speed and number of YES or NO answers.

(+) Can calculate mean speed, and draw a simple conclusion.
(−) Gives no explanation of why individuals estimated speed as they did, a fairly superficial finding.

Exam advice

You need to remember the actual estimated speeds so you can provide a detailed description of the findings.

> ***Describe how the cognitive approach could explain the inaccuracy of eyewitness testimony.***
>
> The cognitive approach explains <u>behaviour</u> in terms of internal mental processes. Therefore it would explain the inaccuracy of eyewitness testimony in terms of how information is handled in our minds.
>
> Loftus and Palmer's study shows that our memories are affected by the language that is used when a memory is encoded. Leading questions bias what is remembered, leading eyewitnesses to remember something they didn't actually witness.

Section A type questions

In Section A of the G542 exam there will always be one question worth 4 marks on the study by Loftus and Palmer (eyewitness testimony).

The questions below give you a taste of the kinds of questions you will be expected to answer on this section of the exam. In the exam each question would specifically mention Loftus and Palmer (eyewitness testimony).

1 (a) Identify the independent variable (IV) and the dependent variable (DV) in the first experiment. **[2]**
   (b) Describe **one** effect this IV had on the dependent variable (DV). **[2]**

2 (a) Identify the IV in the second experiment. **[2]**
   (b) Identify the DV in the second experiment. **[2]**

3 Outline **two** ways the procedure was standardised in the first experiment. **[4]**

4 (a) In the second experiment, there were **two** experimental groups. Identify these groups. **[2]**
   (b) There was a third group in this study, the control group. Explain the purpose of this group. **[2]**

5 Describe **one** strength and **one** weakness of the experimental method used in this study. **[4]**

6 (a) Describe the sample in the second experiment. **[2]**
   (b) Outline **one** difference between the responses given by the two experimental groups in the second experiment. **[2]**

7 Identify **two** pieces of evidence that demonstrate that leading questions can alter a person's perception of events. **[4]**

8 Both experiments involved an independent measures design. Give **one** strength and **one** weakness of using this design in this study. **[4]**

9 Describe the procedure in the second experiment conducted by Loftus and Palmer on eyewitness testimony. **[4]**

10 The first experiment involved a series of questions, one of which was the leading question.
   (a) Explain in what is meant by a 'leading question'? **[2]**
   (b) Explain in what way the question in the experiment was 'leading'? **[2]**

11 In the second experiment, one group of participants had the word 'smashed' in the critical question and the other group had the word 'hit'.
   (a) Which group was more likely to recall broken glass? **[2]**
   (b) Explain why this group was more likely to remember broken glass. **[2]**

12 (a) Outline **one** piece of evidence from the study which supports the suggestion that leading questions can alter a person's memory for events. **[2]**
   (b) Explain in what way this evidence supports the hypothesis that leading questions can alter a person's memory for events. **[2]**

13 Outline **two** ways in which this study can be said to be low in ecological validity. **[4]**

14 (a) Describe how the effect of leading questions was measured. **[2]**
   (b) Suggest **one** problem with measuring leading questions in this way. **[2]**

15 (a) Identify **two** ways that quantitative data was gathered in this study. **[2]**
   (b) Give **two** examples of the quantitative data gathered. **[2]**

16 (a) Describe how the data was collected. **[2]**
   (b) Suggest **one** reason why this data may not be considered valid. **[2]**

17 Outline **two** findings from the second experiment. **[4]**

18 (a) Identify **two** controls used in this study. **[2]**
   (b) Explain why **one** of these controls was used. **[2]**

19 (a) Outline why this study is considered to be an experiment. **[2]**
   (b) Explain why this study is not a field experiment. **[2]**

20 (a) Explain how the sample was obtained in the first study. **[2]**
   (b) Explain **one** strength of obtaining a sample in this way in this study. **[2]**

It is important to actually write out your answers to these questions – you may think you can do them but find, when you try to write down your answer, that in fact you didn't know the answer or didn't know what to write in order to gain the full 2 marks. Better to find that out now than in the exam!

See www.psypress.com/books/ details/9781848721807/ for suggested answers.

Section B type questions

In Section B of the G542 exam you will be asked to provide detailed information about one core study. The questions will be similar to those below. You should practise answering these questions in relation to the study by Loftus and Palmer (eyewitness testimony).

Background and aims

1. Outline previous research related to the study by Loftus and Palmer. **[3]**
2. What was the aim of the study by Loftus and Palmer? **[2]**
3. State **one** hypothesis investigated in this study. **[2]**

Design and procedure

4. Explain why this study can be considered to be a laboratory experiment. **[4]**
5. Suggest **one** strength of using this method in the context of this study. **[3]**
6. Suggest **one** weakness of using this method in the context of this study. **[3]**
7. Explain why it was necessary to do experiment 2? **[2]**
8. Describe the sample used in experiment 1. **[3]**
9. Describe how the sample in this study was selected. **[3]**
10. Suggest **one** strength of using this sample. **[3]**
11. Suggest **one** weakness of using this sample. **[3]**
12. Explain why experiment 1 can be considered a snapshot study. **[4]**
13. With reference to experiment 1, suggest **one** strength of conducting snapshot studies. **[3]**
14. With reference to experiment 1, suggest **one** weakness of conducting snapshot studies. **[3]**
15. Describe **two** ethical issues raised by this study. **[6]**
16. Outline the procedure followed by this study. **[8]**
17. Describe improvements/changes that could be made to this study. **[8]**
18. Evaluate the improvements/changes that you have suggested. **[8]**

Findings

19. Give **two** examples of quantitative data that was collected in this study. **[4]**
20. Suggest **one** strength of the quantitative data collected. **[3]**
21. Suggest **one** weakness of the quantitative data collected. **[3]**
22. Outline the findings of this study. **[8]**
23. Discuss the reliability of the findings of this study. **[6]**
24. Discuss the validity of the conclusions of this study. **[6]**
25. Discuss the ecological validity of this study. **[6]**

Section C type questions

In Section C of the G542 exam there is one question (four parts) on the approaches/perspectives.

1. Outline **one** assumption of the cognitive approach. **[2]**
2. Describe how the cognitive approach could explain eyewitness testimony. **[4]**
3. Describe **one** similarity and **one** difference between the study by Loftus and Palmer and any other study that has followed the cognitive approach. **[6]**
4. Discuss strengths and weaknesses of the cognitive approach using examples from the Loftus and Palmer study. **[12]**

Exam advice for question 10

On page 21 one strength of using the sample is identified. Just stating this strength would not be sufficient for 3 marks. You must always elaborate your answer so context and detail are included, as described on page 17.

Example answer for question 14

An answer is likely to include the following details:

Snapshot studies do not allow the researcher to discover whether results are due to the development of the behaviour or to individual differences.

LINK TO STUDY...

In the Loftus and Palmer study the student participants will have had different experiences especially driving experiences.

Therefore their inability to accurately recall the speed of the vehicles may have been due to individual differences rather than because they had been asked a leading question.

Exam advice for question 17

To answer this question you could consider changes to the sample, the sampling method, materials, measurement, controls, procedure, ethics.

For example, In the Loftus and Palmer study you might use a different kind of sample (older or younger people) and change the controls used (use repeated measures).

Exam advice on question 4

In the actual exam you are not restricted to just one study but can use any study that is relevant to the named approach. There are three cognitive core studies (Loftus and Palmer, Baron-Cohen et al., Savage-Rumbaugh et al.) but you could also use others, such as Samuel and Bryant, Maguire et al. and Griffiths.

Baron-Cohen et al.

Context

Autistic spectrum disorder

This study investigates a possible explanation for **autistic spectrum disorder** (**ASD**) which includes **autism** at one end of the spectrum and **Asperger syndrome** (**AS**) at the other end. All individuals with ASD share certain characteristics (such as a lack of emotional and social skills, and desire for sameness). At the AS end the individuals have normal intelligence and normal language development whereas individuals at the autistic end tend to have learning difficulties (such as low intelligence).

Theory of Mind

It has been suggested that a core feature of ASD is lack of a **Theory of Mind** (**ToM**). In other words, people with ASD lack the ability to understand what is going on in someone else's mind. This is not the same kind of mindreading as actually knowing what someone else is thinking, for example realising that your friend is secretly plotting to steal your boyfriend. ToM is the more everyday ability to understand a person's facial expressions and realise, for example, that they are sad or happy.

Previous research

Baron-Cohen previously conducted research looking at children with autism. He tested ToM using the **Sally–Anne test**, demonstrating that children with autism lacked ToM.

Other studies have tested adults and found that adults with ASD can pass ToM tests such as the Sally–Anne test. However, such tests are designed for children and are not complex tests. Therefore, an adult with ASD who has more general experience but who still lacks ToM may be able to pass such tests.

Where does it all go wrong?

Students often get confused between the four different tasks that participants have to do in this study.

Students also get confused about which tasks were done by which participants.

The following table might help:

Task	Participants		
	Asperger syndrome	Normal	Tourette syndrome
A	x	x	x
B	x		x
C	x		
D	x		

Aim

The aim of this study is to assess the mindreading abilities of high-functioning ASD adults using a new test designed for adults, the *Eyes Task*.

The aim is to support past findings linking autism to a lack of ToM.

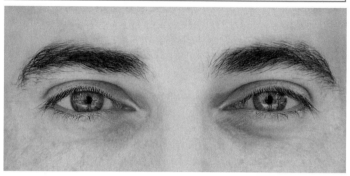

Serious or playful?

Procedure

Task A: Eyes Task

1 Photographs were used of the eye region of 25 different faces (male and female).
2 The photos were taken from magazines and were standardised: same size (15 x 10 cm), all black and white and all of the same region (from midway along the nose to just above the eyebrow).
3 Each picture was shown for three seconds. Participants had to select between two mental state terms printed under each picture.
4 These mental state terms were either 'basic' mental states (such as sad/happy or concerned/unconcerned) or more 'complex' (such as fantasising/noticing or nervous about you/interested in you).

Task B: Strange Stories Task

5 AS and TS participants (Groups 1 and 3) were tested on Happé's *Strange Stories Task*.
6 Participants answered questions on what the characters in the story were thinking and also questions about physical events.

Task C: Gender Recognition of Eyes

7 This was a control task where AS participants (Group 1) just had to identify the gender of the eyes. The task involved face perception but not mindreading.

Task D: Basic Emotion Recognition Task

8 This was another control task. AS participants had to identify basic emotions in whole faces to demonstrate they could recognise emotional states in a simple test.

Sample

Three groups of participants were tested:

- **Group 1**: Participants with autism/AS, normal intelligence, 13 males and three females. This was a **self-selected sample** drawn from an advert in the *National Autistic Society* magazine as well as through doctors.
- **Group 2**: 50 normal adults, age **matched** with individuals in Group 1. This was a **random sample** drawn from a subject panel at the University of Cambridge.
- **Group 3**: Participants with **Tourette syndrome (TS)**, age matched, eight males and two females. This was a self-selected sample from a clinic in London.

Groups 2 and 3 served as controls to see if 'normal' adults could cope with the tasks, and also to see if individuals with other developmental disorders (such as TS) could cope.

(+) Sample included control groups.
(+) Sample used AS adults and therefore could show that AS adults have mindreading deficits as well as autistic children.
(−) Many participants were volunteers.

Research method/technique

This is a **quasi-experiment** as the IV varied naturally. It is an **independent measures** design and a **snapshot** study.

IV = ASD group, 'normal' **control group** and TS control group

DV = Performance on the *Eyes Task* (and other tasks)

Hypothesis = Participants in Group 1 do less well on the *Eyes Task* than the other two groups of participants.

(+) Technique of objective testing reduces bias.
(−) Cannot claim that the IV *caused* change in DV in a quasi-experiment.

Quantitative data e.g. in the *Eyes Task*, there was a numerical score.

(+) Makes it easy to compare the performances of the autism/AS group and the other participants.
(−) Oversimplifies the differences between people with AS and others.

Findings

Task A: Eyes Task

- The autism/AS group did least well, with a **mean** score of 16.3 out of 25.
- The normal and TS groups did about the same, scoring 20.3 and 20.4 respectively.
- The ranges of scores were fairly similar: autism/AS range 13–23, normal and TS range 16–25.
- There was a **ceiling effect** on this task because some participants in the normal and TS groups scored full marks.

Task B: Strange Stories Task

- Group 1 (the individuals with autism/AS) had more difficulty with this task than Group 3 (TS).
- This supports the **validity** of the *Eyes Task* as a test for autism.

Tasks C and D: The control tasks

- Group 1 (autism/AS) performed normally on task C and task D.
- This shows that they could perceive facial features and could identify basic emotion just from seeing someone's eyes. What they couldn't do was interpret what this means in terms of an internal state.

> **Exam advice**
> Answers to this question in the exam must always include the word 'behaviour'.

> *Describe how the cognitive approach could explain the difficulties experienced by individuals with autism.*
>
> The cognitive approach explains <u>behaviour</u> in terms of internal mental processes. Therefore it would explain the difficulties experienced by individuals with autism in terms of a problem with their mental (cognitive) processes, specifically an impaired ToM. This inability to understand what other people are thinking and feeling is proposed as an important component of autism/AS.
>
> For example, in Baron-Cohen *et al.*'s study, high-functioning adults with autism/AS did less well on the *Eyes Task* than 'normal' participants. This suggests that they lack a ToM (a kind of mental activity).

Section A type questions

In Section A of the G542 exam there will always be one question worth 4 marks on the study by Baron-Cohen, Jolliffe, Mortimore and Robertson (autism in adults).

The questions below give you a taste of the kinds of questions you will be expected to answer on this section of the exam. In the exam each question would specifically mention Baron-Cohen, Jolliffe, Mortimore and Robertson (autism in adults).

1 (a) Identify the independent variable (IV) and the dependent variable (DV) in this experiment. **[2]**
   (b) Describe **one** effect the independent variable (IV) had on the dependent variable (DV). **[2]**

2 This study involved three groups of participants. Describe **two** of these groups. **[4]**

3 The table of data below outlines the findings from the *Eyes Task*.

	Mean score on *Eyes Task*
Autism group	16.3
Tourette group	20.3

   (a) Explain what was involved in the *Eyes Task*. **[2]**
   (b) Outline **one** conclusion that can be drawn from this table. **[2]**

4 There was a ceiling effect for the 'normal' participants on the *Eyes Task*.
   (a) Explain what a ceiling effect is. **[2]**
   (b) Explain why this ceiling effect did not influence the conclusions drawn from this study. **[2]**

5 Outline **one** piece of evidence from the study that supports the suggestion that people with autism lack a Theory of Mind. **[4]**

6 Outline **two** ways in which this study can be said to be low in ecological validity. **[4]**

7 (a) Identify **one** difference between the performance of the autistic adults and the Tourette syndrome adults. **[2]**
   (b) Identify **one** of the word pairs in the *Eyes Task*. **[2]**

Sometimes you will find you are giving the same answer to two different questions – that is not uncommon.

8 (a) Outline **two** ways that the *Eyes Task* was standardised. **[2]**
   (b) Aside from the *Eyes Task*, outline **one** other task used in the study. **[2]**

9 (a) Describe the **two** control groups used in this study. **[2]**
   (b) Explain why it was necessary to have control groups. **[2]**

10 (a) Describe how Theory of Mind was measured. **[2]**
   (b) Suggest **one** problem with measuring Theory of Mind in this way. **[2]**

11 (a) Explain **one** method used to collect quantitative data in this study. **[2]**
   (b) Give **two** examples of the quantitative data gathered. **[2]**

12 This participants in each group were age matched.
   (a) Explain what this means. **[2]**
   (b) Explain how the sample with autism were obtained. **[2]**

13 (a) Describe **one** way in which the study lacked ecological validity. **[2]**
   (b) Explain why it was appropriate for this study to lack ecological validity. **[2]**

14 (a) Outline **one** way in which the sample may be considered representative. **[2]**
   (b) Outline **one** way in which the sample may be considered unrepresentative. **[2]**

15 This study was conducted with adults.
   (a) Explain why this particular age group was used in this study. **[2]**
   (b) Identify **two** characteristics of the sample used in this study. **[2]**

16 (a) Identify **two** controls used in this study. **[2]**
   (b) Explain why one of these controls was used. **[2]**

17 (a) Identify **two** criteria used to select the participants in this study. **[2]**
   (b) Explain why the researchers could not manipulate the independent variable (IV). **[2]**

18 (a) Explain what the *Eyes Task* measures. **[2]**
   (b) Explain **one** limitation of using this method. **[2]**

19 (a) Outline why this study is considered to be an experiment. **[2]**
   (b) Explain why this study is not a field experiment. **[2]**

20 The sample of normal adults were randomly selected from a subject panel.
   (a) Explain what this means. **[2]**
   (b) Explain why this sample may be biased. **[2]**

See www.psypress.com/books/details/9781848721807/ for suggested answers.

Section B type questions

In Section B of the G542 exam you will be asked to provide detailed information about one core study. The questions will be similar to those below. You should practise answering these questions in relation to the study by Baron-Cohen, Jolliffe, Mortimore and Robertson (autism in adults).

Background and aims

1 Outline previous research related to the study by Baron-Cohen *et al.* [2]
2 What was the aim of this study? [2]
3 State the hypothesis investigated in this study. [2]

> **Exam advice for question 1**
>
> *This question may be worth 2 or 3 marks – so make sure you adjust your answer accordingly. In this case only 2 marks worth is required.*
>
> *For example:* Baron-Cohen previously conducted research using children. In this previous research Theory of Mind was assessed using the Sally–Anne test. The children with autism were unable to complete this test.

Design and procedure

4 Explain why this study can be considered to be a quasi-experiment. [4]
5 Suggest **one** strength of using this method in the context of this study. [3]
6 Suggest **one** weakness of using this method in the context of this study. [3]
7 Describe the sample used in this study. [3]
8 Explain why **three** different groups were used in this study. [3]
9 Explain how these groups were selected for this study. [3]
10 Suggest **one** strength of using this technique to select participants. [3]
11 Suggest **one** weakness of using this technique to select participants. [3]
12 Explain why this study can be considered a snapshot study. [4]
13 With reference to this study, suggest **one** strength of conducting snapshot studies. [3]
14 With reference to this study, suggest **one** weakness of conducting snapshot studies. [3]
15 Describe **two** ethical issues raised by this study. [6]
16 Outline the procedure followed by this study. [8]
17 Describe improvements/changes that could be made to this study. [8]
18 Evaluate the improvements/changes that you have suggested. [8]

> **Exam advice for question 10**
>
> *Contextualise!*
>
> *Make sure you provide specific information relevant to this study in your answer.*

> **Exam advice for question 17**
>
> *This question part requires candidates to consider the implications of their improvements/changes – in fact it is sometimes phrased as 'Outline the implications of the improvements you have suggested for this study.'*

Findings

19 Give **two** examples of quantitative data that was collected in this study. [4]
20 Suggest **one** strength of the quantitative data collected. [3]
21 Suggest **one** weakness of the quantitative data collected. [3]
22 Outline the findings of this study. [8]
23 Discuss the reliability of the findings of this study. [6]
24 Discuss the validity of the conclusions of this study. [6]
25 Discuss the ecological validity of this study. [6]

Section C type question

In Section C of the G542 exam there is one question (four parts) on the approaches/perspectives.

1 Outline **one** assumption of the cognitive approach. [2]
2 Describe how the cognitive approach could explain the difficulties experienced by individuals with autism. [4]
3 Describe **one** similarity and **one** difference between the study by Baron-Cohen *et al.* and any other study that has followed the cognitive approach. [6]
4 Discuss strengths and weaknesses of the cognitive approach using examples from the Baron-Cohen *et al.* study. [12]

> **Exam advice for question 2**
>
> *When explaining how the cognitive approach can explain autism, always refer to the assumptions of the cognitive approach in your answer.*

Savage-Rumbaugh *et al.*

Context

Past research

A number of researchers, prior to this study, had trained apes in the use of human language. One of the first attempts was by the Hayes who taught their chimpanzee, Vicki, to talk. She did learn four sounds, 'Mama', 'Papa', 'cup' and 'up', but her use of them was not very language-like and the sounds were not very convincing either.

One of the best-known studies of animal language involved a female chimpanzee, Washoe. She was raised by the Gardners and later the Fouts. Washoe was taught to use American Sign Language. It was reported that Washoe could reliably use about 250 signs. The jury is still out on whether Washoe developed language or not. The Gardners pointed to the range of signs and the situations she used them in, but others noted that she never developed a regular word order, which is a basic feature of any language use.

Prior to this core study, Savage-Rumbaugh conducted her own research with two common chimpanzees (*Pan troglodytes*) called Sherman and Austin, who were specifically trained to use lexigrams.

Where does it all go wrong?

This is a difficult study because there is so much information.

It will help you if you make sure you know and understand the following features of the study:

- How 'speech' was recorded (indoors and outdoors).
- How 'speech' was classified (there were four ways).
- How 'speech' was tested (know the formal tests and the findings).
- In addition there was also the question of whether the chimpanzees really meant what they said (see behavioural verification).

Aim

The aim of this research is to investigate the human language capabilities of pygmy chimpanzees.

The key focus of this study is to:

(a) Show that human language capabilities can be acquired with no training.
(b) Demonstrate human language capabilities by showing that the chimpanzees were able to provide differential responses on cue.

Lexigrams were displayed on a computer or on a board. Each symbol brightened when touched. A speech synthesiser was added.

Procedure

Creating the learning environment

1 **Exposure to language** – Kanzi was exposed to the use of lexigrams and human speech from the age of six months as he watched the interactions between his mother (Matata) and her keepers. Mulika learned lexigrams by observing Kanzi. In contrast with Sherman and Austin, Kanzi and Mulika were not trained to use lexigrams.

2 **Outdoor environment** – To get food the chimpanzees had to go to named places in the 55 acre forest.

3 **Indoor environment** – Kanzi and Mulika helped in various activities, e.g. doing the laundry and making food.

Procedures for identifying language use

4 **Lexigram use** indoors was automatically recorded; outdoors it was recorded by hand.

5 **Classification** – Each utterance was classified as (1) accurate (2) spontaneous (3) imitated (4) structured (e.g. initiated by a question or object).

6 **Behavioural verification** – Checking the chimpanzee responded to a symbol in an appropriate way. The reliability of these observations was checked.

Formal testing

7 The testing of all four chimpanzees was carefully controlled to rule out the effect of cueing, e.g. order of items varied so the researcher didn't know what was tested.
  - Shown photograph, asked to select lexigram.
  - Listened to a word, asked to select photograph.
  - Listened to a word, asked to select lexigram.
  - Listened to a synthesised version of the word, asked to select lexigram. (Only Kanzi was tested with synthesised voice.)

Sample

The report concerns four chimpanzees, an **opportunity sample**:

Participant 1. Kanzi, a pygmy chimpanzee (Bonobo chimpanzee or *Pan paniscus*). He was aged 30–47 months during the time of this report.

Participant 2. Mulika, Kanzi's younger sister. She was aged 11–21 months during the period of this report.

Participants 3 and **4.** Austin and Sherman, who belonged to the order 'common chimpanzees' (*Pan troglodytes*). They had been previously trained and studied by Savage-Rumbaugh. This report uses these two common chimpanzees as a point of comparison.

(+) Bonobos are very social and highly intelligent, which suggests they would be most likely to develop language.

(−) Kanzi and Mulika were not 'normal' bonobos – they had been reared from birth in a 'language environment' and also might have been especially intelligent chimpanzees, so therefore not representative.

Research method/technique

This study is a **longitudinal case study**, spanning 17 months.

(+) A tremendous amount of detail relating to language acquisition could be gathered.

(−) The researchers may have become emotionally involved with the chimpanzees and therefore lacked objectivity in the way they interpreted the chimpanzees' behaviour.

Findings

Imitation and spontaneous use of symbols

- Kanzi first started using lexigrams after his mother left (age 17 months), including banana, chase, peanut, Austin. He must have learned these by watching Matata use symbols (imitation).
- Mulika started using the lexigrams earlier (at 12 months). At first a word like 'milk' was just an all-purpose instruction to be picked up or for food.
- During the period covered by the report, Kanzi acquired 46 words and Mulika 37 words.
- In 17 months Kanzi produced 2,540 non-imitative combinations, plus 265 which were prompted or partially imitated.
- For both Kanzi and Mulika, about 15% of utterances were imitation and 80% were spontaneous (i.e. not prompted).
- Both chimpanzees used a new term in an associative context first, similar to children, i.e. labelling an object in its original context. Referential and representative use came later.
- Kanzi was able to lead a visitor at the Language Learning Centre who knew nothing of the forest to the various sites on request.

Formal tests

- All the four chimpanzees could match photographs to lexigrams.
- Only Kanzi and Mulika could select the appropriate lexigram or photograph when prompted with the spoken word.
- Kanzi was the only one tested with the synthesised voice and did less well than with the spoken voice.

Quantitative data e.g. number of words acquired, percentage imitated.
(+) Makes it easy to compare the performances.
(−) Gives no explanation of the underlying processes in language acquisition.

Qualitative data e.g. the way Kanzi and Mulika used words (associative context first).
(+) Provides insights into the underlying processes in language acquisition.
(−) Makes it difficult to draw simple conclusions about language usage.

Describe how the cognitive approach could explain symbol acquisition in pygmy chimpanzees

The cognitive approach explains behaviour in terms of internal mental processes. Therefore it would explain symbol acquisition in terms of the mental structures in an individual's mind. One assumption is that language is uniquely human and therefore other animals simply do not have the mental structures to be able to learn to manipulate symbols/use human language.

Savage-Rumbaugh's study suggests that this assumption is not true because chimpanzees were able to spontaneously acquire the use of symbols.

Section A type questions

In Section A of the G542 exam there will always be one question worth 4 marks on the study by Savage-Rumbaugh *et al.* (symbol acquisition by pygmy chimpanzees).

The questions below give you a taste of the kinds of questions you will be expected to answer on this section of the exam. In the exam each question would specifically mention Savage-Rumbaugh *et al.* (symbol acquisition by pygmy chimpanzees).

1   (a)   Explain why pygmy chimpanzees were selected for this study. **[2]**
    (b)   How did Austin and Sherman differ from the pygmy chimpanzees? **[2]**

2   Identify **two** pieces of evidence that suggest pygmy chimpanzees have a greater aptitude for symbol acquisition than common chimpanzees. **[4]**

3   (a)   Identify **one** reason why Kanzi was taught symbol acquisition as a means of communication. **[2]**
    (b)   Outline **one** way in which the researchers recorded Kanzi's symbol acquisition. **[2]**

4   Describe how it was decided whether a symbol should be listed as part of Kanzi's vocabulary. **[4]**

5   (a)   Identify **two** ways that qualitative data was gathered in this study. **[2]**
    (b)   Give **two** examples of the qualitative data gathered. **[2]**

6   Describe **two** of the formal tests conducted by Savage-Rumbaugh *et al.* to assess Kanzi's language acquisition. **[4]**

7   Describe how Kanzi and Mulika's symbol use was classified. **[4]**

8   The reliability of observations was checked. Explain how this may have been done. **[4]**

9   (a)   Outline **one** finding from this study. **[2]**
    (b)   Explain **one** conclusion that can be drawn from this finding. **[2]**

10 (a)   What were the names of the **two** pygmy chimpanzees studied? **[2]**
    (b)   Explain why these pygmy chimpanzees may not have been representative of their own species. **[2]**

11 (a)   Identify **two** symbols Kanzi identified correctly using the lexigram keyboard before any training. **[2]**
    (b)   Explain why Kanzi was able to identify these symbols without training. **[2]**

12 Outline **one** piece of evidence from the study that supports the suggestion that animals can acquire human language capabilities with no training. [**[4]**

13 (a)   Identify **one** difference between the performance of the common chimpanzees and the pygmy chimpanzees. **[2]**
    (b)   Identify **two** of symbols on the lexigram. **[2]**

14 (a)   Describe the control group used in this study. **[2]**
    (b)   Explain why it was necessary to have a control group. **[2]**

15 (a)   Describe **one** way that symbol acquisition was measured. **[2]**
    (b)   Suggest **one** problem with measuring symbol acquisition in this way. **[2]**

16 The four chimpanzees in this study all had different experiences in terms of their exposure to symbols. Explain these differences. **[4]**

17 (a)   Describe how the data was collected. **[2]**
    (b)   Suggest **one** reason why this data may not be considered valid. **[2]**.

18 (a)   Describe **one** way in which the study lacked ecological validity. **[2]**
    (b)   Explain why it was appropriate for this study to lack ecological validity. **[2]**

19 (a)   Outline **one** way in which the sample may be considered representative. **[2]**
    (b)   Outline **one** way in which the sample may be considered unrepresentative. **[2]**

20 (a)   Outline why this study is considered to be a case study. **[2]**
    (b)   Explain why this study is considered to be longitudinal. **[2]**

*See www.psypress.com/books/
details/9781848721807/ for suggested answers.*

Section B type questions

In Section B of the G542 exam you will be asked to provide detailed information about one core study. The questions will be similar to those below. You should practise answering these questions in relation to the study by Savage-Rumbaugh *et al.* (symbol acquisition by pygmy chimpanzees).

Background and aims

1   Outline previous research related to the study by Savage-Rumbaugh *et al.* [3]
2   What was the aim of the study by Savage-Rumbaugh *et al.*? [2]

Design and procedure

3   Explain why this study can be considered to be a case study. [4]
4   Suggest **two** advantages of using this method in the context of this study. [3]
5   Suggest **two** disadvantages of using this method in the context of this study. [3]
6   Describe the sample used in this study. [3]
7   Explain why **two** different groups were used in this study. [3]
8   Explain how **one** of these groups was selected for this study. [3]
9   Suggest **one** strength of using this technique to select participants. [3]
10 Suggest **one** weakness of using this technique to select participants. [3]
11 Explain why this study can be considered a longitudinal study. [4]
12 With reference to this study, suggest **one** strength of conducting longitudinal studies. [3]
13 With reference to this study, suggest **one** weakness of conducting longitudinal studies. [3]
14 Describe **two** ethical issues raised by this study. [6]
15 Outline the procedure followed by this study. [8]
16 Describe improvements/changes that could be made to this study. [8]
17 Evaluate the improvements/changes that you have suggested. [8]

Findings

18 Give **two** examples of quantitative data that was collected in this study. [4]
19 Suggest **one** strength of the quantitative data collected. [3]
20 Suggest **one** weakness of the quantitative data collected. [3]
21 Outline the findings of this study. [8]
22 Discuss the reliability of the findings of this study. [6]
23 Discuss the validity of the conclusions of this study. [6]
24 Discuss the ecological validity of this study. [6]

Example answer for question 17

On page 23 there is advice on answering question 17, but what about evaluating your improvements/changes? In this type of question you are required to consider the impact your changes would have.

For example, if you suggest that a different species of primate might be used, you might evaluate this by saying:

If we used gorillas in a future study they might be just as competent, or even more competent, than Kanzi and Mulika. This would show that the original finding is not a fluke but also generalises to other species. It might also be that the new sample would develop even more sophisticated language skills, such as acquiring a bigger vocabulary.

Example answer for question 22

The following points might be included in such an answer:

When the chimpanzees used a lexigram indoors, a computer automatically and objectively recorded symbol usage, eliminating the possibility of human error making findings unreliable.

The researchers classified each utterance as (a) correct or incorrect (b) spontaneous, imitated or structured. Different researchers may have made slightly different judgements about such categorisations that might mean the findings are unreliable.

Section C type questions

In Section C of the G542 exam there is one question (four parts) on the approaches/perspectives.

You should answer these questions in relation to the behaviourist perspective as well.

1   Outline **one** assumption of the cognitive approach. [2]
2   Describe how the cognitive approach could explain symbol acquisition in pygmy chimpanzees. [4]
3   Describe **one** similarity and **one** difference between the study by Savage-Rumbaugh *et al.* and any other study that has followed the cognitive approach. [6]
4   Discuss strengths and weaknesses of the cognitive approach using examples from the Savage-Rumbaugh *et al.* study. [12]

Samuel and Bryant

Aim

The aim of this study is to investigate whether younger children demonstrate a better grasp of conservation if they are asked one question instead of two.

Rose and Blank (1974) previously tested this but only looked at the number tasks and only tested six-year-old children. This study looked at other conservation tasks and a wider age range of participants.

Context

Piaget's theory

The Swiss psychologist Jean Piaget developed a theory of how children's thinking changes as they get older. Before Piaget, psychologists believed that children were the same as adults but just had less knowledge. Piaget suggested that they actually think in a different way. They move from one stage to the next when they are 'ready' – which partly results from experiences in the world but is mainly driven by maturation.

One of Piaget's stages of development is called pre-operational stage (18 months to about seven years) and one of the characteristics of this stage is the inability to conserve quantity (**conservation**). For example, children do not comprehend that if you change the shape of an object it keeps the same mass.

Around the age of seven, Piaget claimed, children acquire the ability to conserve. This stage of development is called the concrete operational stage.

Piaget's conservation task

Piaget demonstrated the inability to conserve using the conservation task, described in the picture above right. The picture shows conservation of volume.

Piaget found that children under the age of about seven years could not conserve, supporting his theory. However, Piaget's methods were criticised because of the way he asked the questions. Margaret Donaldson argued that the use of two questions might confuse children (Piaget asked the same question twice: *Are they the same?*). Children might think they had to give a different answer the second time.

In Piaget's standard conservation task a child is first shown two equal quantities, such as volume (above) or number of counters. They are asked Are they the same? Then the display is transformed in front of the child by pouring the liquid from one glass into a taller, thinner one. Then children are asked a second time, Are they the same?

Procedure

Number of questions

The children were divided into three **experimental conditions**:

1 **Standard condition**, as used by Piaget, where the key question *Are they the same?* was asked twice.
2 **One question** asked, as used by Rose and Blank, where the key question was only asked after the transformation of the display.
3 **Fixed array** was a control condition where the key question was asked once and there was no transformation.

Age

4 Four age groups were tested. Each age group was subdivided into the three task groups above.

Materials

Each child was tested four times on each of the three materials (= 12 tests):

5 **Mass** – Children were shown a Plasticine cylinder, which was then transformed by being made flatter (and thus looked as if there was more).
6 **Number** – A row of counters, which was then transformed by being spread out so the row was longer.
7 **Volume** – A glass filled with water, which was then transformed by being poured into a taller thinner beaker so the water level was higher.

Where does it all go wrong?

Students muddle this study with the next study by Bandura *et al.* and include gender as one of the IVs.

Students also get muddled about the three IVs:

- Number of times the question was asked.
- Age.
- Conservation task: materials used.

Sample

252 boys and girls aged between 5 and 8½ years were tested.

The children were from Crediton in Devon, England; an **opportunity sample**.

The children were divided into four age groups, whose **mean** ages were:

- five years three months
- six years three months
- seven years three months
- eight years three months

(+)   Children of various ages were used, so researchers were able to note how conservation skills develop with age.

(–)   The sample was limited to children from one area of the UK and may not generalise.

Research method/technique

One part of this study is a **laboratory experiment** using **independent measures** (for the condition) and **repeated measures** (for materials). It is a **snapshot** study.

IV = Condition (standard, one question and control); materials

DV = Errors made (i.e. not conserving quantity)

Hypothesis = Participants make more errors in the standard condition than the one-question condition.

There is an association between errors and the materials used.

The study was also a **quasi-experiment** with **independent measures**.

IV = Age

DV = Success on conservation tasks

Hypothesis = Younger children make more errors than older children.

(+)   A laboratory experiment allows cause and effect to be identified, showing that the form of questioning *caused* different levels of performance.

(–)   This was a snapshot study where comparisons were made between children of different ages; it does not control for **participant variables**.

Quantitative data e.g. the number of errors made, mean for each age group.

(+)   Makes it easy to compare the performance of different age groups on conservation tasks.

(–)   Oversimplifies the differences.

Findings

Condition differences

- Children made fewest errors (mean for each child = 4) when asked only one question compared to a mean of 5 errors in the standard condition.
- In the fixed array condition they made most errors (mean per child = 6). This shows that children who conserved must have been using information from the pre-transformation display in order to answer the final question correctly (because the fixed array group did not have this information).

Age

- Younger children made more errors than older children.
- Children in the five-year-old age group scored a mean of 8.1 errors across all conditions whereas the eight-year-olds made 2.1 errors.
- Children aged six made 5.5 errors on average and children aged seven made 3.6 errors.

Age and condition

- For every condition the youngest children made most errors and errors decreased with age.
- For all age groups (except the seven-year-olds) the children performed better on the one-question condition than the standard, two-question condition.

Materials

- Children made fewer errors on the number task (mean = 4.0) and most on the volume task (mean = 5.9).

Describe how the developmental approach could explain why one child can conserve whilst another cannot

The developmental approach explains behaviour as a consequence of age and/or experience. The developmental approach would explain conservation in terms of age – as children get older and mature mentally, their cognitive abilities develop so they can cope with and understand increasingly complex phenomena.

This was shown through Samuel and Bryant's conservation experiment where the mean number of errors made by children in all three conditions decreased with age. In other words, their ability to conserve got increasingly better as they got older. Younger children were able to cope better than Piaget had demonstrated but there were still **significant** developmental differences consistently associated with age.

Section A type questions

In Section A of the G542 exam there will always be one question worth 4 marks on the study by Samuel and Bryant (conservation).

The questions below give you a taste of the kinds of questions you will be expected to answer on this section of the exam. In the exam each question would specifically mention Samuel and Bryant (conservation).

1   There were three independent variables (IVs) in this study.
   (a)   Describe **one** of the independent variables (IVs). **[2]**
   (b)   Outline **one** conclusion that was drawn related to this independent variable (IV). **[2]**

2   Describe **two** of the conservation tasks the children were asked to perform. **[4]**

3   Outline **two** of the experimental conditions. **[4]**

4   One of the independent variables (IVs) in this study was the conservation task.
   (a)   Describe the dependent variable (DV) used with this IV. **[2]**
   (b)   Describe **one** effect the independent variable (IV) had on the dependent variable (DV). **[2]**

5   (a)   Identify **two** features of the sample used. **[2]**
   (b)   Outline **one** possible strength of the sample used. **[2]**

6   (a)   Outline **two** ways that the conservation task was standardised. **[2]**
   (b)   Explain why it is necessary to standardise tasks. **[2]**

7   (a)   Describe **one** control group used in this study. **[2]**
   (b)   Explain why it was necessary to have control groups. **[2]**

8   The findings from this study included the following data related to the one-question condition:

Age	5	6	7	8
Mean number of errors	7.3	4.3	2.5	1.3

   (a)   Outline **one** conclusion that can be drawn from this table. **[2]**
   (b)   Explain the purpose of the 'one-question' group. **[2]**

9   (a)   Identify **two** ways that quantitative data was gathered in this study. **[2]**
   (b)   Give **two** examples of the quantitative data gathered. **[2]**

10   In the study by Samuel and Bryant there was a condition called the 'one-question condition'.
   (a)   Identify the **two** other conditions. **[2]**
   (b)   Explain the purpose of **one** of these conditions. **[2]**

11   Outline **two** conclusions from Samuel and Bryant's study into conservation. **[4]**

12   This study was conducted with children aged between five and eight.
   (a)   Explain why this particular age group was used in this study. **[2]**
   (b)   Outline **one** difficulty that may arise when psychologists study children. **[2]**

13   (a)   Describe **one** piece of evidence that supports Piaget's theory of cognitive development. **[2]**
   (b)   Describe **one** piece of evidence that challenges Piaget's theory of cognitive development. **[2]**

14   (a)   Describe how the participants' age affected their ability to conserve. **[2]**
   (b)   Describe how the type of task affected the participants' ability to conserve. **[2]**

15   (a)   Explain how you could assess the reliability of the conservation task. **[2]**
   (b)   Explain how you could assess the validity of the conservation task. **[2]**

16   Outline **two** ways in which this study can be said to be low in ecological validity. **[4]**

17   Identify **two** differences between the performance of the five-year-old children and the eight-year-old children. **[4]**

18   (a)   Describe how the ability to conserve was measured. **[2]**
   (b)   Suggest **one** problem with measuring conservation in this way. **[2]**

19   (a)   Identify the experimental design used in this study. **[2]**
   (b)   Outline **one** weakness of using this design in this study. **[2]**

20   (a)   Identify **two** criteria used to select the participants in this study. **[2]**
   (b)   Explain why the researchers could not manipulate all of the independent variables (IVs). **[2]**

See
www.psypress.com/books/details/
9781848721807/ for suggested answers.

Section B type questions

In Section B of the G542 exam you will be asked to provide detailed information about one core study. The questions will be similar to those below. You should practise answering these questions in relation to the study by Samuel and Bryant (conservation).

Background and aims

1. Outline previous research related to the study by Samuel and Bryant. **[3]**
2. What was the aim of the study by Samuel and Bryant? **[2]**
3. State **one** hypothesis investigated in this study. **[2]**

Design and procedure

4. Explain why this study can be considered to be a quasi-experiment. **[4]**
5. Suggest **one** strength of using this method in the context of this study. **[3]**
6. Suggest **one** weakness of using this method in the context of this study. **[3]**
7. Describe the sample used in this study. **[3]**
8. Describe how the sample was obtained in this study. **[3]**
9. Explain how the sample in this study was selected. **[3]**
10. Suggest **one** strength of using this sample. **[3]**
11. Suggest **one** weakness of using this sample. **[3]**
12. Explain why this study can be considered a snapshot study. **[4]**
13. With reference to this study, suggest **one** strength of conducting snapshot studies. **[3]**
14. With reference to this study, suggest **one** weakness of conducting snapshot studies. **[3]**
15. Describe **two** ethical issues raised by this study. **[6]**
16. Outline the procedure followed by this study. **[8]**
17. Describe improvements/changes that could be made to this study. **[8]**
18. Evaluate the improvements/changes that you have suggested. **[8]**

Findings

19. Give **two** examples of quantitative data that was collected in this study. **[4]**
20. Suggest **one** strength of the quantitative data collected. **[3]**
21. Suggest **one** weakness of the quantitative data collected. **[3]**
22. Outline the procedure followed by this study. **[8]**
23. Discuss the reliability of the findings of this study. **[6]**
24. Discuss the validity of the conclusions of this study. **[6]**
25. Discuss the ecological validity of this study. **[6]**

> **Example answer for question 4**
>
> *An answer is likely to include the following details:*
>
> *A quasi-experiment has an independent variable (IV) that has not been manipulated by the researcher.*
>
> **LINK TO STUDY...**
>
> *In this study one of the IVs was the age of the child (5, 6, 7, 8). The effect of this IV was observed on a dependent variable (DV), being the children's ability to conserve number, mass and volume.*

> **Exam advice for question 18**
>
> *When considering the implications of improvements (i.e. evaluating your changes) you might include:*
>
> - *Advantages/disadvantages of any changes.*
> - *Increased/decreased naturalness of behaviour recorded.*
> - *Increased/decreased control.*
> - *Improved reliability.*
> - *Improved generalisability.*
> - *Improved usefulness.*
> - *Cost and time implications.*

> **Exam advice for question 23**
>
> *Reliability concerns measurements – so consider how reliable any measurements were.*

Section C type questions

In Section C of the G542 exam there is one question (four parts) on the approaches/perspectives.

1. Outline **one** assumption of the developmental approach. **[2]**
2. Describe how the developmental approach could explain why one child can conserve whilst another cannot. **[4]**
3. Describe **one** similarity and **one** difference between the study by Samuel and Bryant and any other study that has followed the developmental approach. **[6]**
4. Discuss strengths and weaknesses of the developmental approach using examples from the Samuel and Bryant study. **[4]**

> **Exam advice for question 3**
>
> *There are three core studies in the section on developmental psychology, but you could argue that some of the other core studies illustrate the developmental approach and could use those (e.g. Savage-Rumbaugh et al.).*

Bandura *et al.*

Context

Learning theory

The **behaviourist** perspective in psychology suggests that all behaviour is learned directly through experience. Behaviourist explanations are called 'learning theory' and include:

- **Classical conditioning**: We are born with certain stimulus–response links such as salivating when we smell food. If a noise (like a cupboard opening) becomes associated with the likelihood of food, then the animal learns a new stimulus–response link: cupboard opening causes the animal to salivate. Watch any cat.

- **Operant conditioning**: Any action that produces pleasant consequences (rewards, such as warmth or praise or money) is likely to be repeated. Any action that produces unpleasant consequences is less likely to be repeated.

Social learning theory

Behaviourists suggested that rewards have to be experienced directly (i.e. you receive the reward yourself). Albert Bandura suggested that learning can occur when rewards are experienced indirectly. This is called 'social learning' because it involves watching other people (social activity).

This was supported by research. For example, studies have shown that children imitate a behaviour in the immediate environment where they see it happening. For example, if a child sees someone being aggressive to a particular toy then the child will also behave aggressively towards that toy.

However, a more crucial test of imitative (social) learning is to see whether a child will generalise the imitative response patterns to new settings when the model is absent: in other words, whether they will still display the newly learned behaviour in a new setting when the model is no longer present. This is a more crucial test of the principles of imitative learning (or **social learning theory**).

A Bobo doll is an inflatable doll about five feet tall. There is a weight in the bottom that makes it bob back up when it is knocked down.

Aim

The aim of this study is to investigate whether children will imitate aggression.

Specifically to demonstrate the following predictions:

1   Observing an aggressive model will lead a participant to reproduce aggressive acts similar to their models.
2   Observing an aggressive model will lead a participant to behave in a generally more aggressive manner.
3   Participants will imitate the behaviour of a same-sex model to a greater degree than a model of the opposite sex.
4   Boys will be more likely than girls to imitate aggressive behaviour because it is a highly masculine activity.

Where does it all go wrong?

Students sometimes forget:

- There is a non-aggressive model.
- There is a no-model condition.
- Children are tested one at a time
- There are three IVs (see facing page).
- Observations used three behavioural categories.

Procedure

Phase 1: Modelling

1   The children played in an experimental room, watching a **model** playing with toys including a Bobo doll.
2   The children were placed in one of three groups:
  - **Experimental group** 1: Observed an aggressive model who sat on Bobo, punched it, etc.
  - Experimental group 2: Non-aggressive model.
  - **Control group**: No model was present while the children were playing.
3   Children watched a male or female model.

Phase 2: Aggression arousal

4   The children were taken to another room where they were then allowed to play with some attractive toys.
5   This play was abruptly stopped in order to make the children feel frustrated.

Phase 3: Tested for delayed imitation

6   The children were taken to third room where they were observed playing with toys, including the Bobo doll.
7   Each child was observed through a **one-way mirror** by the male model. A second observer was present for half of the participants to determine **inter-rater reliability**.
8   **Observations** were recorded using **behavioural categories**:
  - Imitative aggression, e.g. sitting on Bobo or saying '*Pow*' (actions of the model).
  - Partially imitative, e.g. using mallet on toys other than Bobo.
  - Non-imitative aggression, e.g. punching Bobo doll, saying hostile things not said by the model.
  - Aggressive gun play.

Sample

The participants were children from a university nursery school in Stanford, California; an **opportunity sample.**

There were 36 boys and 36 girls in the sample, aged between 37 and 69 months (approximately three to five years).

The **mean** age was 52 months (about 4½ years).

Matched pairs design: Aggressiveness (a potential **extraneous variable**) was controlled by ensuring that each group contained equally aggressive children. Aggressiveness ratings of the children were determined beforehand by an experimenter who knew the children well and one of the children's teachers.

Research method/technique

This is a **laboratory experiment** using **observational techniques**. It is an **independent measures** design and a **snapshot** study.

IVs = Aggressive or non-aggressive model, gender of model, gender of child

DV = Imitation of aggressive acts/behaviour observed in playroom

Hypotheses = See predictions on facing page.

(+) Participants were all children, which allowed Bandura to show how easily youngsters imitate adult models.
(−) Participants were American children; it might be that children who live in a less violent society might be less willing to imitate anti-social behaviour.

(+) The controlled environment and manipulation of IVs allowed conclusions about how observation causes imitation.
(−) **Demand characteristics** may explain the children's behaviour – the Bobo doll 'invited' children to behave aggressively.

Findings

Imitation of aggression

- **Complete imitation** Children in the aggressive condition imitated many of the models' physical and verbal behaviours (e.g. saying 'Pow'), both aggressive and non-aggressive behaviours.
  In contrast, children in the non-aggressive and control conditions displayed very few aggressive behaviours (70% of them had zero scores).
- **Partial imitation** There were differences for partial imitation in the same direction as those found for complete imitation.
- **Non-imitative aggression** The aggressive group displayed more non-imitative aggression than the non-aggressive group, though the difference was small and not **significant**.
- **Non-aggressive behaviour** Children in the non-aggression condition spent more time playing non-aggressively with dolls than children in the other groups.

Gender effects

- **Same-sex imitation** There was some evidence of a 'same-sex effect' for boys but not for girls.
- **Gender of model** The male models had a greater influence in general than the female models.
- **Gender of child** Boys imitated more physical aggression than girls but the groups didn't differ in terms of verbal aggression.

Quantitative data e.g. the number of aggressive behaviours displayed.
(+) Makes it easy to compare the performance of the two groups.
(−) Gives no explanation of why they imitated the behaviour

Qualitative data e.g. the kinds of imitation that were made.
(+) Provides insight about how models affected aggressive behaviour.
(−) Makes it difficult to draw simple conclusions.

> *Describe how the developmental approach could explain why one child is aggressive whereas another child is not*
>
> The developmental approach explains <u>behaviour</u> as a consequence of age and/or experience. Therefore it would explain how children learn to be aggressive as they grow older through exposure to social learning processes. Children observe models' behaviour and may later imitate this. This is called **observational learning**.
>
> In Bandura *et al.*'s study the children tended to imitate the aggressive behaviour. Children may be more likely to imitate a behaviour if they identify with the model. This may happen when a boy observes a man performing the behaviour. This was the case in Bandura's study where boys were more likely to imitate a model if it was a man.

Section A type questions

In Section A of the G542 exam there will always be one question worth 4 marks on the study by Bandura, Ross and Ross (aggression).

The questions below give you a taste of the kinds of questions you will be expected to answer on this section of the exam. In the exam each question would specifically mention Bandura, Ross and Ross (aggression).

1   One of the independent variables (IVs) in this study was the behaviour of the model (aggressive or non-aggressive).
  (a)   Identify the other **two** independent variables (IVs) in this study. **[2]**
  (b)   Describe the effect of **one** of these IVs on the dependent variable (DV). **[2]**

2   (a)   Identify the **two** experimental groups in this study. **[2]**
  (b)   Outline **one** finding from this study. **[2]**

3   This study used a 'matched pairs' experimental design.
  (a)   Explain why the children were matched in this study. **[2]**
  (b)   Outline how the children were matched in this study. **[2]**

4   Two independent variables (IVs) were related to gender.
  (a)   Identify **one** other independent variable (IV) and **one** dependent variable (DV). **[2]**
  (b)   Outline how the independent variable (IV) was manipulated in this experiment. **[2]**

5   In the first part of this experiment the children watched a model playing with toys. Explain what happened in the second part. **[4]**

6   In the final part of the study the children were observed playing with toys.
  (a)   Explain why this was necessary. **[2]**
  (b)   Outline how this observation was conducted. **[2]**

7   (a)   What was the dependent variable (DV) in this study? **[2]**
  (b)   Describe **two** of the categories used to assess the dependent variable (DV). **[2]**

8   The participants in this study were children.
  (a)   Identify **two** other characteristics of the sample used in this study. **[2]**
  (b)   Outline **one** difficulty that may arise when psychologists study children. **[2]**

9   Outline **two** findings from this study. **[4]**

10   Describe **two** ethical problems in this study. **[4]**

11   Outline **one** piece of evidence from the study that supports the suggestion that aggression can be learned through observation. **[4]**

12   Outline **two** ways in which this study can be said to be low in ecological validity. **[4]**

13   (a)   Identify the experimental design used in this study. **[2]**
  (b)   Outline **one** weakness of using this design in this study. **[2]**

14   (a)   Describe how aggression was measured. **[2]**
  (b)   Suggest **one** problem with measuring aggression in this way. **[2]**

15   (a)   Describe the control group used in this study. **[2]**
  (b)   Explain why it was necessary to have control groups. **[2]**

16   In this study, all the participants were taken individually into a second room and subjected to mild aggression arousal.
  (a)   Describe how the children's aggression was aroused in this room. **[2]**
  (b)   Explain why the researcher felt this was necessary. **[2]**

17   Observations were made of the children's aggressive behaviour.
  (a)   Explain how the reliability of these observations was evaluated. **[2]**
  (b)   Outline **one** conclusion from this study. **[2]**

18   (a)   Outline **one** way in which the sample may be considered representative. **[2]**
  (b)   Outline **one** way in which the sample may be considered unrepresentative. **[2]**

19   This study was conducted with children.
  (a)   Explain why this particular age group was used in this study. **[2]**
  (b)   Explain why the findings might have been different if adults were used. **[2]**

20   (a)   Give **two** examples of quantitative data that was collected in this study. **[2]**
  (b)   Suggest **one** strength of the quantitative data collected. **[2]**

See www.psypress.com/ books/details/9781848721807/ for suggested answers.

Section B type questions

In Section B of the G542 exam you will be asked to provide detailed information about one core study. The questions will be similar to those below. You should practise answering these questions in relation to the study by Bandura, Ross and Ross (aggression).

Background and aims

1   Outline previous research related to the study by Bandura *et al.* **[3]**
2   What was the aim of the study by Bandura *et al*? **[2]**
3   State **one** hypothesis investigated in this study. **[2]**

Design and procedure

4   Explain why this study can be considered to be a laboratory experiment. **[4]**
5   Suggest **one** strength of using this method in the context of this study. **[3]**
6   Suggest **one** weakness of using this method in the context of this study. **[3]**
7   Describe the sample used in this study. **[3]**
8   Explain why matching was necessary in this study. **[3]**
9   Explain how the sample in this study was matched. **[3]**
10 Suggest **one** strength of using this sample. **[3]**
11 Suggest **one** weakness of using this sample. **[3]**
12 Explain why this study can be considered a snapshot study. **[4]**
13 With reference to this study, suggest **one** strength of conducting snapshot studies. **[3]**
14 With reference to this study, suggest **one** weakness of conducting snapshot studies. **[3]**
15 Describe **two** ethical issues raised by this study. **[6]**
16 Outline how observation was used in this study. **[6]**
17 Outline the procedure followed by this study. **[8]**
18 Describe improvements/changes that could be made to this study. **[8]**
19 Evaluate the improvements/changes that you have suggested. **[8]**

Findings

20 Give **two** examples of qualitative data that was collected in this study. **[4]**
21 Suggest **one** strength of the qualitative data collected. **[3]**
22 Suggest **one** weakness of the qualitative data collected. **[3]**
23 Outline the findings of this study. **[8]**
24 Discuss the reliability of the findings of this study. **[6]**
25 Discuss the validity of the conclusions of this study. **[6]**
26 Discuss the ecological validity of this study. **[6]**

> **Exam advice for question 1**
>
> *This question is not often asked in the exam but it obviously pays to be prepared with some knowledge about previous research.*

> **Exam advice for question 16**
>
> *Sometimes specific procedures are required, as in question 16 here.*
>
> *A good answer would contain plenty of detail such as:*
>
> - *The number and position of the observers.*
> - *The frequency of the observations.*
> - *The categories that were used.*

> **Exam advice for question 17**
>
> *'Procedure' only refers to what the researchers did during the study itself and excludes sampling.*

> **Exam advice for question 18**
>
> *Just a reminder about these questions – 8 marks is a lot of marks so you need to practise doing these well.*
>
> *You can consider changes to the sample, the sampling method, materials, measurement, controls, procedure, ethics.*
>
> *'Less is more' – don't tackle all possible changes, just select a few but make sure you thoroughly describe how you would make those changes. If you do less, you'll have time to provide detail.*

Section C type questions

In Section C of the G542 exam there is one question (four parts) on the approaches/perspectives.

1   Outline **one** assumption of the developmental approach. **[2]**
2   Describe how the developmental approach could explain why one child is aggressive whereas another child is not. **[4]**
3   Describe **one** similarity and **one** difference between the study by Bandura *et al.* and any other study that has followed the developmental approach. **[6]**
4   Discuss strengths and weaknesses of the developmental approach using examples from the Bandura *et al.* study. **[12]**

> *You should answer questions 1–4 on Bandura et al. in relation to the behaviourist perspective as well.*

Freud

Context

In the nineteenth and twentieth centuries Sigmund Freud developed a theory of personality and a theory of the origins of mental disorder.

Freud's theory of personality

Freud proposed that adult personality is shaped by childhood events. He considered that children go through various stages of development, such as the oral stage and the anal stage. At each stage a child needs to resolve certain conflicts in order for healthy psychological development to continue.

In the third stage of development, the **phallic stage**, the child's focus is on their genitals. This occurs around the age of four. Freud proposed that boys desire their mothers and regard their fathers as a rival, wishing them dead. Freud called this the **Oedipus complex.** The boy's wish that the father was dead creates anxiety. It is eventually resolved when a boy comes to identify with his father.

Freud's theory of mental disorder

Freud proposed that mental illness can be explained in terms of **ego defence mechanisms** – techniques we use to protect ourselves from a full awareness of unpleasant thoughts and feelings. For example, **repression** is the blocking of unacceptable feelings or memories from consciousness. Such defence mechanisms are not fully effective and our unconscious thoughts are expressed through, for example, dreams or maladaptive behaviours such as **phobias.**

Psychoanalysis

The term **psychoanalysis** is used to refer to Freud's theory of personality development and also a form of therapy – his 'talking cure'. As a form of therapy, psychoanalysis aims to help patients become consciously aware of their unconscious, repressed feelings. By consciously acknowledging these feelings the patient can accept them and recover.

Freud suggested to Hans that his fear of horses might be related to the fact that they symbolised his father. The black around the horses' mouths and the blinkers in front of their eyes might represent of his father's moustaches and glasses.

Aim

The aim of this study is to document the case of Little Hans who was suffering from anxiety that led to a phobia.

Freud's aims were to use the case study to support his ideas about:

- Child development and the Oedipus complex.
- The origins of mental disorders such as phobias.
- The value of psychoanalysis for treating mental disorder.

Where does it all go wrong?

There is an important distinction between findings and conclusions – when asked an exam question about findings, the conclusions may not always be creditworthy.

But in this case study the conclusions can be considered as part of the findings as they are reported by Hans' father as evidence.

Useful exam advice … know the details of at least one of the dreams or fantasies.

Procedure

1   The data in this case study was written down by Hans' father. He became concerned about his son's fear of horses and discussed the matter with Freud. His association with Freud was because he was one of Freud's closest 'followers', a member of Freud's Wednesday night study group.

2   Hans' father sent regular reports to Freud about the case. The written record was similar to a diary, kept over a period of years.

3   The final record published by Freud consisted of data collected in the following ways:
- A factual record of events in Hans' family life, such as the birth of his sister and the time when Hans heard a father warn his daughter about touching a white horse. These events were noted down by Hans' father.
- **Observations** of Hans' behaviour made by his father, such as Hans' behaviour with his 'widdler' (penis).
- Conversations between Hans and his father, noted down by Hans' father.
- Both Freud and Hans' father analysed the events that unfolded and included their comments in the written record. For example, Freud suggested that a horse represented Hans' father. Hans' father often suggested what the boy might be thinking.

4   On one occasion during the case study Hans was taken to meet Freud. (Freud also met Hans later in the boy's life.)

Sample

The study concerns one boy, 'Little Hans', during the time from when he was between three and five years old.

His family members (father, mother and sister) form an important part of the study.

Hans and his family were selected because Hans' father was interested in Freud's work and wished to give Freud the opportunity to explore his theories about the origin of phobias and psychosexual development. It is an **opportunity sample**.

E

(+) A unique opportunity for an in-depth study of a boy in the phallic stage of development who had developed a phobia.
(−) Hans' phobia and character (he was a particularly nervous child) were unique so we cannot generalise the findings to other fears and phobias.

Research method/technique

This is a **case study** of a single individual. It is a **longitudinal** design spanning two years.

E

(+) Focusing on one individual means a lot of detail could be gathered about his fears, dreams and fantasies.
(−) The close involvement of both Hans' father and Freud meant the study lacked objectivity.
(−) Hans may have responded to his father's questions in the desired way because he wished to please his father and/or the questions were **leading questions**.

E

Qualitative data e.g. the comments made by Little Hans.
(+) Provides rich, in-depth insight into his experiences, thoughts and feelings that can be analysed to explain his phobias.
(−) More open to bias and subjective interpretation than **quantitative data**.

Findings

Part I: Early life

- Hans had a need to repress certain anxieties: his desire to have a sexual relationship with his mother (Oedipus complex), and his wish for his father and sister to die because they were rivals for his mother.
- Hans developed a fascination with his 'widdler' because he was in the phallic stage, and a desire for his mother because of the Oedipus complex.

Part II: Analysis

- Hans' fear of horses can be explained in terms of ego defences. His mother told him his penis would be cut off if he touched it. Hans repressed the anxiety this created but the anxiety was expressed in a fear of horses that might bite if you touched them.
- Hans' fear of horses was also explained by Freud as a subconscious fear of his father (see facing page). He was fearful of his father because of the Oedipus complex.
- Hans' fear of carts was explained because they represented pregnancy, which was related to his anxieties about his sister.
- Hans' daydream about giraffes was interpreted as a representation of him trying to take his mother away from his father so he could have her to himself – another feature of the Oedipus complex.

Part III: Resolution

- Hans' fantasy about the plumber was interpreted as him now identifying with his father, having passed through the Oedipus complex.
- Hans' fantasy of becoming a father (and his father was then the granddaddy) was a resolution of his Oedipus complex because now both he and his father were married to his mother.

Describe how the psychodynamic perspective could explain phobias

The psychodynamic perspective explains <u>behaviour</u> in terms of unconscious thoughts and feelings. Therefore it would explain phobias in terms of feelings that have been repressed into the unconscious mind.

In the case of Little Hans his anxieties about his feelings for his mother and father cause him anxiety, so he repressed them. These unconscious feelings became attached to horses because his father looked like a horse and also represented the instruction not to touch certain things. The link between horses and anxiety led Hans to be very scared of them.

Describe how the developmental approach could explain phobias

The developmental approach explains <u>behaviour</u> as a consequence of age and/or experience. Therefore it would explain Hans' phobias (and their disappearance) in terms of his experiences as he got older.

Section A type questions

In Section A of the G542 exam there will always be one question worth 4 marks on the study by Freud (Little Hans).

The questions below give you a taste of the kinds of questions you will be expected to answer on this section of the exam. In the exam each question would specifically mention Freud (Little Hans).

1   Freud's study of Little Hans is used to illustrate the phallic stage of development.
   (a)   Explain the importance of this stage of development. **[2]**
   (b)   Give **one** example of Hans' behaviour that was an example of this stage of development. **[2]**

2   Outline **one** strength and **one** weakness of the way in which the data was gathered. **[4]**

3   Little Hans is referred to as a 'little Oedipus'.
   (a)   Identify **two** features of the Oedipus complex. **[2]**
   (b)   Outline **one** piece of evidence from the study that supports this suggestion. **[2]**

4   (a)   Explain Hans' feelings towards his mother. **[2]**
   (b)   Explain Hans' feelings towards his sister. **[2]**

5   (a)   Briefly describe **one** of Little Hans' dreams or fantasies. **[2]**
   (b)   Outline Freud's explanation of this dream or fantasy. **[2]**

6   Freud believed that Hans' phobia of horses was triggered by real events.
   (a)   Describe **one** event that may have triggered Hans' phobia. **[2]**
   (b)   Explain how this event might have been linked to Hans' unconscious anxieties. **[2]**.

7   (a)   Explain why this sample was chosen. **[2]**
   (b)   Outline **one** way in which the sample may be considered unrepresentative. **[2]**

8   Describe **two** conclusions that can be drawn from this study. **[2]**

9   (a)   Describe **one** of Hans' phobia of horses. **[2]**
   (b)   Describe Freud's interpretation of **one** of Hans' phobias. **[2]**

10   Describe why Freud suggested that Hans' fear of horses symbolised his fear of his father. **[4]**

11   (a)   Describe how the data was collected in this study. **[2]**
   (b)   Suggest **one** reason why this data may not be considered valid. **[2]**

12   Hans' father interpreted Hans' dream about the giraffes.
   (a)   Outline the interpretation of this dream. **[2]**
   (b)   Suggest **one** problem with the way Hans' father interpreted the dream. **[2]**

13   Outline **one** piece of evidence from the study that supports Freud's ideas about the development of mental illness. **[4]**

14   (a)   Outline Hans' feelings about his sister. **[2]**
   (b)   Give **one** piece of evidence that supports these feelings. **[2]**

15   At the end of the study, Hans had a fantasy about becoming a father.
   (a)   Outline this fantasy. **[2]**
   (b)   Explain how this fantasy helped him pass through the Oedipus complex. **[2]**

16   Consider the following conversation:

   Father: Did you often get into bed with your Mummy?
   Hans: Yes

   (a)   Give **one** problem with this kind of questioning. **[2]**
   (b)   Explain why Hans may have wished to get into bed with his mother. **[2]**

17   Outline **two** ethical problems that may arise when psychologists study children. **[2]**

18   (a)   Give **one** piece of evidence that shows that Little Hans wished to be married to his mother. **[2]**
   (b)   Give **one** piece of evidence that shows that Hans' mother rejected his approaches. **[2]**

19   Outline **two** methods that were used to collect data in this study. **[4]**

20   (a)   Explain why Hans was chosen to be the subject of this case study. **[2]**
   (b)   Describe **one** limitation of using Hans as the subject of this case study. **[2]**

*See www.psypress.com/books/
details/9781848721807/ for suggested answers.*

Section B type questions

In Section B of the G542 exam you will be asked to provide detailed information about one core study. The questions will be similar to those below. You should practise answering these questions in relation to the study by Freud (Little Hans).

Background and aims

1   Outline previous research related to the study by Freud. **[3]**

2   What was the aim of the study by Freud? **[2]**

Design and procedure

3   Explain why this study can be considered to be a case study. **[4]**

4   Suggest **one** strength of using this method in the context of this study. **[3]**

5   Suggest **one** weakness of using this method in the context of this study. **[3]**

6   Describe why the sample was used in this study. **[3]**

7   Explain how the sample in this study was selected. **[3]**

8   Suggest **one** strength of using this sample. **[3]**

9   Suggest **one** weakness of using this sample. **[3]**

10   Explain why this study can be considered a longitudinal study. **[4]**

11   With reference to this study, suggest **one** strength of conducting longitudinal studies. **[3]**

12   With reference to this study, suggest **one** weakness of conducting longitudinal studies. **[3]**

13   Describe **two** ethical issues raised by this study. **[6]**

14   Outline the procedure followed by this study. **[8]**

15   Describe improvements/changes that could be made to this study. **[8]**

16   Evaluate the improvements/changes that you have suggested. **[8]**

Findings

17   Give **two** examples of qualitative data that was collected in this study. **[4]**

18   Suggest **one** strength of the qualitative data collected. **[3]**

19   Suggest **one** weakness of the qualitative data collected. **[3]**

20   Outline the findings of this study. **[8]**

21   Discuss the reliability of the findings of this study. **[6]**

22   Discuss the validity of the conclusions of this study. **[6]**

23   Discuss the ecological validity of this study. **[6]**

> **Example answer for question 12**
>
> *Freud's study was longitudinal because it spanned several years.*
>
> *A strength of a longitudinal study is that it enables one to see changes in the participant's behaviour.*
>
> **LINK TO STUDY...**
>
> *Freud had the time to study Hans' phobia of horses. He made suggestions about the meaning of Hans' phobias (they represented a fear of his father whose moustache and glasses resembled the black around a horse's mouth and the blinkers worn over a horse's eyes). The fact that these interpretations led to a change in Hans' behaviour supported the accuracy of the interpretations.*

> **Exam advice for question 21**
>
> *This question requires you to report the findings of this study – sometimes the term 'results' is used but they mean the same thing.*
>
> *In the case of this study the findings/results include the interpretation of the evidence – as that is part of the evidence provided. Usually 'interpretation' = conclusions, not findings.*

Section C type questions

In Section C of the G542 exam there is one question (four parts) on the approaches/perspectives.

1   Outline **one** assumption of the developmental approach. **[2]**

2   Describe how the developmental approach could explain phobias. **[4]**

3   Describe **one** similarity and **one** difference between the study by Freud and any other study that has followed the developmental approach. **[6]**

4   Discuss strengths and weaknesses of the developmental approach using examples from the Freud study. **[12]**

> *You should answer questions 1–4 on Freud in relation to the psychodynamic perspective as well – as this case study is a prime example of that approach.*

Maguire *et al.*

Aim

The aim of this study is to investigate the role of the hippocampus in spatial memory and navigation.

Specifically:

• To see whether the brain is capable of changing in response to environmental stimulation.
• To identify the precise role of the hippocampus.
• To demonstrate structural changes in the human brain in response to behaviour requiring spatial memory.

Context

The hippocampus

The hippocampus is a small component of the brain. There is one hippocampus on each side (i.e. one in each hemisphere), located deep inside the temporal lobe. The temporal lobes are on the sides of the brain.

Spatial memory

Many birds and small animals have a need for spatial memory. For example they need it to find food they have hidden – they have to remember where they put it and find their way there again.

Research has shown that the hippocampus is central to spatial memory. For example, in species that have a need for spatial memory the hippocampi are larger than in species with less need for spatial memory (when overall brain and body size are taken into account).

Further evidence comes from research which found that, in some animals, the size of the hippocampi (hippocampal volume) increases during seasons when they use their spatial memory most.

Where does it all go wrong?

Get the results right →

	Left hippocampus	Right hippocampus
Anterior		CONTROL
Body		CONTROL
Posterior	TAXI DRIVERS	TAXI DRIVERS

Also ... understand the role of the 50 participants used for baseline data.

Procedure

Image analysis method 1: VBM

1   VBM is '*voxel-based morphometry*'. A 'voxel' is a volumetric pixel i.e. a pixel with three dimensions (height, width and depth). A *pixel* is a single point on a graphic image ('pixel' stands for pix + element).
2   This technique measures the volume of specific brain areas by comparing each brain area to a template. MRI scans were made of 50 healthy male brains to produce the template (an average of all the brains scanned).
3   VBM identifies differences in the density of the grey matter in a person's brain (grey matter is grey because it is dense in neural connections).
4   VBM is an automatic procedure that uses Statistical Parametric Mapping.

Image analysis method 2: Pixel counting

5   MRI scans were made of slices through the hippocampi (see diagram on left).
6   The slices produce two-dimensional pictures.
7   The images were analysed by one person who counted the pixels in each slice to produce a measure of hippocampal volume by adding up the number of pixels in all slices.
8   This person was 'blind' to (i.e. didn't know) whether a participant was a taxi driver or a non-taxi driver, and also 'blind' to the VBM findings.

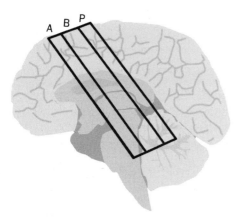

Brain slices used for pixel counting.

The diagram above shows where the photographic slices were taken through the brain. The slices cut through the length of the hippocampus covering three regions:

A – anterior hippocampus (6 slices)

B – body hippocampus (12 slices)

P – posterior hippocampus (6 slices)

Sample

London taxi drivers were used because their work involves spatial memory and navigation. It is an **opportunity sample**.

Experimental group: 16 right-handed, male taxi drivers who had passed the test 'The Knowledge' (rigorous test).

- **Mean** age was 44 years (range 32–62 years).
- Mean experience of taxi driving 14.3 years (range 1.5–42 years).
- Mean training time was two years (range 10 months – 3.5 years).
- All had healthy medical, neurological and psychiatric profiles.

Matched control group

The experimental group was matched by health, mean age, age range, gender and handedness with 16 non-taxi drivers drawn from a pool of 50 men whose records were held in a structural MRI scan database.

(+) Participants had extensive need to use spatial memories.
(−) Unique characteristics of the sample (e.g. male, right-handed, Londoners) means that findings may not generalise.

Research method/technique

This is a **quasi-experiment** as the IV varied naturally, using **independent measures**. It is a **snapshot** study.

IV = Taxi driving (use of spatial memory) or not

DVs = Hippocampal volume in four areas: right and left, anterior and posterior hippocampi

Hypothesis = The hippocampi of taxi drivers are different to the hippocampi of the control group.

(+) Enables study of an IV that cannot be manipulated.
(−) Hippocampus size not controlled e.g. some members of the control group may have been engaged in activities using spatial memory, or members of the **experimental group** may have been born with larger hippocampi.

Quantitative data e.g. number of pixels.
(+) Provides objective, unbiased data to enable comparisons to be made between groups of participants.
(−) Oversimplifies memory processes by focusing on size of brain regions, whereas the way they are connected may be more important.

Exam advice

Questions on findings may be worth 8 marks, so identify 8 findings. Don't forget DETAIL is important.

Findings

Results from VBM

- There was **significantly** more grey matter in both left and right hippocampi (LH and RH) of taxi drivers than controls.
- This difference was only in the posterior portion of both RH and LH.
- In contrast, the controls had relatively more grey matter in the anterior RH and LH.
- No differences were observed elsewhere in the brain.

Results from pixel counting

- Total hippocampal volumes and intercranial volume did not differ significantly between taxi drivers and non-taxi drivers.
- In the control group the anterior RH and the body of the RH were larger (i.e. had more volume) than taxi drivers.
- In the taxi driver group both the posterior RH and LH had greater volume than in the controls.

Changes with navigational experience

- There was a **positive correlation** between time spent taxi-driving and volume of the posterior RH.
- There was a **negative correlation** between time and the volume of the anterior RH and LH.

Describe how the physiological approach could explain why some people have better spatial memories

The physiological approach explains <u>behaviour</u> in terms of processes in the body and the brain. Therefore it would explain spatial memories in terms of the way they are stored in the brain.

Maguire *et al.*'s study showed that people who used their spatial memory a lot (taxi drivers) had more brain cells in one region of the hippocampus – the posterior portion. This suggests that experience does affect the organisation of the brain.

Since there was a correlation between time spent as a taxi driver and hippocampal volume, this suggests that the number of cells increase when they are needed.

Section A type questions

In Section A of the G542 exam there will always be one question worth 4 marks on the study by Maguire *et al.* (taxi drivers).

The questions below give you a taste of the kinds of questions you will be expected to answer on this section of the exam. In the exam each question would specifically mention Maguire *et al.* (taxi drivers).

1 (a) Identify the independent variable (IV) and the dependent variable (DV) in this experiment. **[2]**
   (b) Describe **one** effect the independent variable (IV) had on the dependent variable (DV). **[2]**

2 This study used an independent measures design.
   (a) Describe **one** limitation of this design in this study. **[2]**
   (b) Explain why Maguire *et al.* could not manipulate the independent variable (IV). **[2]**

3 (a) Describe **two** features of the sample. **[2]**
   (b) Outline **one** limitation of this sample. **[2]**

4 (a) Identify the **two** techniques used to analyse the MRI scans. **[2]**
   (b) Outline **one** difference between the MRI scans of the taxi drivers and non-taxi drivers. **[2]**

5 (a) Explain why taxi drivers and non-taxi drivers were used. **[2]**
   (b) Identify **two** criteria used to select the taxi drivers in this study. **[2]**

6 (a) Outline the function of the hippocampus as described in this study. **[2]**
   (b) Outline **one** finding that supports this function. **[2]**

7 (a) Identify **two** controls used in this study. **[2]**
   (b) Explain why it was important to use controls in this study. **[2]**

8 (a) Explain **one** method used to measure the size of the hippocampi in this study. **[2]**
   (b) State **one** problem with measuring hippocampal size in this way. **[2]**

9 Outline **one** piece of evidence from the study that supports the role of the hippocampus in spatial memory. **[4]**

10 (a) Explain how an MRI scan was used in this study. **[2]**
   (b) Outline **one** piece of evidence that suggests the brains of taxi drivers are different from the brains of non-taxi drivers. **[2]**

11 A negative correlation was found between time spent driving and the volume of the anterior hippocampi.
   (a) Explain what a negative correlation is in the context of this study. **[2]**
   (b) Give **one** conclusion that can be drawn from this finding. **[2]**

12 A positive correlation was calculated between volume change in the right posterior hippocampus and time as a taxi driver.
   (a) Explain **one** conclusion that can be drawn from this. **[2]**
   (b) Give **one** limitation of using a correlation. **[2]**

13 One method used to measure hippocampal volume was pixel counting.
   (a) Briefly explain what is involved in this method. **[2]**
   (b) Give **one** reason why the data collected may be considered to be reliable. **[2]**

14 This study involved two groups of participants. Describe both groups. **[4]**

15 (a) Identify **two** criteria used to select the participants in this study. **[2]**
   (b) Identify **one** difference between the hippocampal size of the taxi drivers and non-taxi drivers. **[2]**

16 One method used to assess hippocampal volume was voxel-based morphometry.
   (a) Explain why this method involved a template. **[2]**
   (b) Explain how this template was produced. **[2]**

17 There was no difference in the total hippocampal volume of taxi drivers and non-taxi drivers.
   (a) Explain this finding. **[2]**
   (b) Give **one** reason why the data may not be considered to be valid. **[2]**

18 (a) Outline **one** way in which the sample may be considered representative. **[2]**
   (b) Outline **one** way in which the sample may be considered unrepresentative. **[2]**

19 (a) In this study what group of participants acted as a control group? **[2]**
   (b) Why is it necessary to have a control group? **[2]**

20 (a) What conclusion can be drawn about spatial memory from this study? **[2]**
   (b) Give **one** piece of evidence to support this conclusion. **[2]**

See www.psypress.com/ books/details/9781848721807/ for suggested answers.

Section B type questions

In Section B of the G542 exam you will be asked to provide detailed information about one core study. The questions will be similar to those below. You should practise answering these questions in relation to the study by Maguire *et al.* (taxi drivers).

Background and aims

1 Outline previous research related to the study by Maguire *et al*. **[3]**

2 What was the aim of the study by Maguire *et al*.? **[2]**

3 State the hypothesis investigated in this study. **[2]**

Design and procedure

4 Explain why this study can be considered to be a quasi-experiment. **[4]**

5 Suggest **one** strength of using this method in the context of this study. **[3]**

6 Suggest **one** weakness of using this method in the context of this study. **[3]**

7 Describe the sample used in this study. **[3]**

8 Explain why **two** different samples were used in this study. **[3]**

9 Explain how the sample in this study was selected. **[3]**

10 Suggest **one** strength of using this sample. **[3]**

11 Suggest **one** weakness of using this sample. **[3]**

12 Explain why this study can be considered a snapshot study. **[4]**

13 With reference to this study, suggest **one** strength of conducting snapshot studies. **[3]**

14 With reference to this study, suggest **one** weakness of conducting snapshot studies. **[3]**

15 Describe **two** ethical issues raised by this study. **[6]**

16 Outline the procedure followed by this study. **[8]**

17 Describe improvements/changes that could be made to this study. **[8]**

18 Evaluate the improvements/changes that you have suggested. **[8]**

Findings

19 Give **two** examples of quantitative data that was collected in this study. **[4]**

20 Suggest **one** strength of the quantitative data collected. **[3]**

21 Suggest **one** weakness of the quantitative data collected. **[3]**

22 Outline the findings of this study. **[8]**

23 Discuss the reliability of the findings of this study. **[6]**

24 Discuss the validity of the conclusions of this study. **[6]**

25 Discuss the ecological validity of this study. **[6]**

> **Exam advice for question 5**
>
> *Contextualise!*
>
> *On page 45 one strength of using the experimental method is identified. Just stating this strength would not be sufficient for 3 marks. You must always elaborate your answer so context and detail are included, as described on page 17.*

> **Example answer for question 23**
>
> *The following points might be included in such an answer:*
>
> • *MRI scanners can be used repeatedly in the same way and therefore give accurate, consistent data.*
>
> • *VBM is a scientific technique which automatically enables every point of the brain to be examined in an objective and unbiased way.*
>
> • *The pixel counting was only conducted by one individual who, although experienced in the technique, may have made errors.*
>
> • *Only 24 photographic slices of each brain were used in the final analysis, possibly not enough to ensure reliability.*

Section C type questions

In Section C of the G542 exam there is one question (four parts) on the approaches/perspectives.

1 Outline **one** assumption of the physiological approach. **[2]**

2 Describe how the physiological approach could explain why some people have better spatial memories. **[4]**

3 Describe **one** similarity and **one** difference between the study by Maguire *et al*. and any other study that has followed the physiological approach. **[6]**

4 Discuss strengths and weaknesses of the physiological approach using examples from the Maguire *et al*. study. **[12]**

> **Exam advice on question 3**
>
> *You can really select any aspect of the two studies here, such as looking at the samples used by Maguire* et al. *and another named study using the physiological approach.*

Dement and Kleitman

Context

Sleep

Sleep is a very active state, both physically and mentally. Our bodies move frequently and our brain activity is even more varied during sleep than it is during the normal waking state.

REM sleep

Different stages of sleep have been identified. One way to classify the stages is on the basis of eye movements. At certain times during the night a person's eyes dart about under closed eyelids. This is called rapid eye movement sleep or **REM sleep**.

REM sleep is also characterised by a lack of muscle tone, resulting in a temporary paralysis (which explains why you sometimes can't move in a dream). REM sleep has sometimes been called 'paradoxical sleep' because the eyes and brain are active but the body is paralysed except for the eyes.

This stage is also associated with a unique **brain wave** pattern – fast, desynchronised electrical activity in the brain that resembles the state of the awake brain.

Research has found that people in REM sleep are likely to be dreaming, so this might provide a very useful way of knowing when someone is dreaming and would permit the objective study of dreams.

NREM sleep refers to sleep when there is no rapid eye movement – non-rapid eye movement.

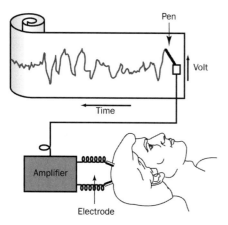

How an EEG recording is made: electrical activity is picked up by electrodes and translated into a series of wavy lines representing the amount of volts being produced in the brain at any time. A 'brain wave' is the rapid alternation between high and low voltage.

Aim

The aim of this study is to conduct a rigorous assessment of the relationship between REM sleep and dreams. This relationship can be determined by answering certain questions:

- Do dreams occur just in REM sleep or also during quiet sleep (NREM sleep)?
- Is there a positive correlation between the length of an REM episode and how long a person thought they were dreaming?
- Does the pattern of eye movements during REM relate to the visual experience of a dream?

Where does it all go wrong?

Students often forget the correlation study (see facing page, top right, in the research methods box).

The main study is an *association*, not a cause-and-effect experiment. The only conclusion that can be drawn is that REM sleep is associated with dreaming, rather than suggesting that REM sleep causes dreaming. This is because REM sleep cannot be manipulated.

Procedure

1   Participants were observed in a sleep **laboratory** while they slept. They were told to eat normally but abstain from drinks containing alcohol or caffeine on the day of the study.
2   Their eye movements were recorded through the night by attaching electrodes to their eyes and recording movement with an **EOG** (electro-oculograph).
3   Their brain waves were recorded through the night by attaching electrodes to their scalp. Electrical activity was recorded using an **EEG** (electroencephalograph).
4   The participants went to bed in a quiet, dark room. They were awoken by a bell at various intervals, either in REM or NREM sleep, and asked to speak into a recording machine near the bed (this was used to prevent any cueing from the researcher). They were asked to report:
- Whether they had been dreaming, and if so ...
- The content of the dream.
- Whether they were dreaming for 5 or 15 minutes.
5   When they had finished speaking the experimenter occasionally entered the room to further question them on some particular point of the dream. They were then allowed to go back to sleep.
6   They were also awoken during episodes of vertical or horizontal eye movement and asked to describe their dream.
7   Of the five participants who were studied intensively:
- Two were woken using a table of **random** numbers.
- One was woken during three REM periods and three NREM periods.
- One was told he would be woken only during REM but in fact was woken randomly during REM and NREM.
- One was woken at the whim of the researcher.
8   No participants were told whether they had just been having REM activity when they were woken.

Sample

There were nine adults in total: seven adult males and two females. All were American. It is an **opportunity sample**.

Five of the participants were studied intensively and referred to by their initials (DN, IR, KC, WD, PM).

E

(+) A range of different individuals were studied rather than just one **case study**.
(–) Small sample size, all American adults, therefore not generalisable.

Research method/technique

This is a **controlled observation** conducted in a **laboratory**.

It is also a **quasi-experiment** as the IV varied naturally.

IV = REM or NREM sleep

DV = Number of times dreams reported

Hypothesis = More dreams are reported in REM sleep than NREM sleep.

Parts of the study were a **correlation**.

Correlation hypothesis = There is a positive correlation between the estimate of time spent dreaming and the duration of REM sleep.

E

(+) Conducting a controlled observation means that **extraneous variables** can be excluded (such as factors which might disturb a person's sleep at home).
(–) In a laboratory people may have different sleep patterns to normal.

Findings

Occurrence of REM activity

- On average REM activity lasted 20 minutes and occurred every 92 minutes.
- The frequency was characteristic for each individual.
- Episodes tended to be longer later on in the night.

REM versus NREM activity

- Participants frequently reported having a dream when woken during REM sleep (65–90% of the time) but were less likely to report a dream in NREM sleep (3–12.5%).
- Most of recall in NREM periods was within eight minutes of the end of an REM episode.

Length of REM periods and dream duration estimates

- Participants were 83% correct in estimating whether REM activity lasted for 5 or 15 minutes.
- There were **significantly** more correct estimates of length of REM than incorrect estimates (92 correct, 19 incorrect).
- There was a significant positive correlation between the duration of REM activity and the number of words used to describe a dream.

Eye movement patterns and visual imagery of dream

- There was a strong association between pattern of REMs and the content of dreams. For example, horizontal eye movements during REM sleep were linked in one participant to a dream about two people throwing tomatoes.

E

Quantitative data e.g. number of dreams in REM and NREM, estimate of dream duration.
(+) Provides easy means to analyse differences between REM and NREM.
(–) May oversimplify the difference between the two – may be fewer dreams in NREM but they might be more complex.

Qualitative data e.g. content of dreams.
(+) Enables understanding of link between dream content and physical changes (eye movement).
(–) Less objective, so can be affected by researcher's expectations.

Describe how the physiological approach could explain dreaming

The physiological approach explains behaviour in terms of processes in the body and the brain. Therefore it could explain dreaming in terms of brain activity.

Dement and Kleitman showed that there was an association between a particular brain state (REM sleep) and the subjective experience of dreaming. When people were awaken during REM sleep they were more likely to report having a dream than if they were awoken during NREM sleep. Dement and Kleitman also found that subjective experiences were related to the actual eye movement, for example if someone reported they were dreaming about throwing tomatoes it was observed that their eyes had been moving horizontally.

Section A type questions

In Section A of the G542 exam there will always be one question worth 4 marks on the study by Dement and Kleitman (sleep and dreaming).

The questions below give you a taste of the kinds of questions you will be expected to answer on this section of the exam. In the exam each question would specifically mention Dement and Kleitman (sleep and dreaming).

1   (a)   Identify the independent variable (IV) and the dependent variable (DV) in this quasi-experiment. **[2]**
    (b)   Describe **one** way that the dependent variable (DV) was measured in this study. **[2]**

2   (a)   Identify **two** substances participants were told not to have on the day of the study. **[2]**
    (b)   Outline **one** problem with instructing the participants not to have these substances. **[2]**

3   Dement and Kleitman used an electroencephalograph (EEG) machine.
    (a)   Explain what an EEG measures. **[2]**
    (b)   Describe **one** limitation of using an EEG to investigate dreaming. **[2]**

4   Dement and Kleitman used an electro-oculograph (EOG).
    (a)   Explain what an EOG measures. **[2]**
    (b)   Describe **one** limitation of using an EOG to investigate dreaming. **[2]**

5   (a)   Identify **two** controls used in this study. **[2]**
    (b)   Explain why **one** of these controls was used. **[2]**

6   Controlled observations were made in this study.
    (a)   Describe the controlled observations. **[2]**
    (b)   Give **one** strength of using this technique. **[2]**

7   (a)   Identify **two** characteristics of REM sleep. **[2]**
    (b)   Explain why it is not possible to manipulate the independent variable (IV) in this study. **[2]**

8   Describe **two** pieces of evidence from this study that support a link between REM (rapid eye movement) sleep and dreaming. **[4]**

9   (a)   Outline **one** way in which the sample may be considered representative. **[2]**
    (b)   Outline **one** way in which the sample may be considered unrepresentative. **[2]**

10 (a)   Outline **two** ways that procedure was standardised. **[2]**
    (b)   Explain why standardisation is important. **[2]**

11 It is suggested that rapid eye movements (REM) only occur during dreaming. Give **one** piece of evidence that supports this suggestion and **one** piece of evidence that challenges it. **[4]**

12 (a)   Identify **two** characteristics of the sample used in this study. **[2]**
    (b)   Suggest how these characteristics may have affected the findings. **[2]**

13 (a)   Describe **one** way in which the study lacked ecological validity. **[2]**
    (b)   Explain why it was appropriate for this study to lack ecological validity. **[2]**

14 (a)   Identify **one** of the hypotheses in this study. **[2]**
    (b)   Outline the results in relation to this hypothesis. **[2]**

15 Participants were asked to estimate the duration of their dream.
    (a)   How did the researchers collect this data? **[2]**
    (b)   What evidence was produced from this part of the study? **[2]**

16 It was suggested that dreaming in NREM sleep was actually 'leftovers' from REM sleep.
    (a)   Outline **one** piece of evidence to support this. **[2]**
    (b)   Identify **one** characteristic of NREM sleep aside from the lack of rapid eye movements. **[2]**

17 A positive correlation was calculated between the number of words used to describe a dream and the duration of REM activity.
    (a)   What is shown by a positive correlation? **[2]**
    (b)   Suggest **one** problem with assuming that REM sleep is the same as dreaming. **[2]**

18 Participants were occasionally awoken when their eye movements were either horizontal or vertical and asked to report the content of their dream.
    (a)   Give **one** example of a dream reported when eye movements were mainly vertical. **[2]**
    (b)   Give **one** example of a dream reported when eye movements were mainly horizontal. **[2]**

19 (a)   Give **one** reason why the data in this study may not be considered to be reliable. **[2]**
    (b)   Give **one** reason why the data in this study may not be considered to be valid. **[2]**

20 (a)   Outline why this study is considered to be an experiment. **[2]**
    (b)   Explain why this study is a laboratory experiment. **[2]**

See www.psypress.com/books/details/9781848721807/ for suggested answers.

Section B type questions

In Section B of the G542 exam you will be asked to provide detailed information about one core study. The questions will be similar to those below. You should practise answering these questions in relation to the study by Dement and Kleitman (sleep and dreaming).

Background and aims

1 Outline previous research related to the study by Dement and Kleitman. **[3]**
2 What was the aim of the study by Dement and Kleitman? **[2]**
3 State **one** hypothesis investigated in this study. **[2]**

Exam advice for question 3

There are no extra marks for writing two hypotheses.

Design and procedure

4 Explain why this study can be considered to be a quasi-experiment. **[4]**
5 Suggest **one** strength of using this method in the context of this study. **[3]**
6 Suggest **one** weakness of using this method in the context of this study. **[3]**
7 Describe the sample used in this study. **[3]**
8 Explain how the sample in this study was selected. **[3]**
9 Suggest **one** strength of using this sample. **[3]**
10 Suggest **one** weakness of using this sample. **[3]**
11 Describe **two** ethical issues raised by this study. **[6]**
12 Outline the procedure followed by this study. **[8]**
13 Describe improvements/changes that could be made to this study. **[8]**
14 Evaluate the improvements/changes that you have suggested. **[8]**

Exam advice for question 13

Just another reminder that 'less is more'.

One improvement to this study might be to increase the sample size – but how many participants would be desirable? What kind of participants? Young and old perhaps, or from a different cultural group? By providing the answers to questions like this you are supplying all-important detail (see comments about marking criteria on page 17).

Findings

15 Outline how qualitative data was collected in this study. **[2]**
16 Give **two** examples of qualitative data that was collected in this study. **[4]**
17 Suggest **one** strength of the qualitative data collected. **[3]**
18 Suggest **one** weakness of the qualitative data collected. **[3]**
19 Give **two** examples of quantitative data that was collected in this study. **[4]**
20 Suggest **one** strength of the quantitative data collected. **[3]**
21 Suggest **one** weakness of the quantitative data collected. **[3]**
22 Outline the findings of this study. **[8]**
23 Discuss the reliability of the findings of this study. **[6]**
24 Discuss the validity of the conclusions of this study. **[6]**
25 Discuss the ecological validity of this study. **[6]**

Exam advice for question 15

Sometimes questions about qualitative data ask about how it was collected in the study instead of asking for examples.

Make sure you answer the right question!

An example of the 'how' answer would be:

Qualitative data was gathered by waking participants and instructing them to first state whether or not they had been dreaming, and then, if they could, to relate the content of the dream into a tape recorder. This information was later analysed.

Section C type questions

In Section C of the G542 exam there is one question (four parts) on the approaches/perspectives.

1 Outline **one** assumption of the physiological approach. **[2]**
2 Describe how the physiological approach could explain sleep and dreaming. **[4]**
3 Describe **one** similarity and **one** difference between the study by Dement and Kleitman and any other study that has followed the physiological approach. **[6]**
4 Discuss strengths and weaknesses of the physiological approach using examples from the Dement and Kleitman study. **[4]**

Exam advice on questions 1 and 2

Answers in the exam must always include the word 'behaviour'.

Aim

The aim of this study is to record the psychological effects of hemispheric disconnection in patients with severe epilepsy.

The aim is also to use the results to understand how the right and left hemispheres work in 'normal' individuals.

Apparatus used in studying split-brain patients.

Context

Hemispheres of the brain

The brain is divided into two halves called **hemispheres**. The right hemisphere and left hemisphere (RH and LH) of the brain communicate with each other via a small group of connections. The main connection is the **corpus callosum**. There are also some smaller connections – the anterior commisure, hippocampal commisure and the massa intermedia.

The importance of communication between the hemispheres is that otherwise you have, in essence, two brains that can function independently. However, there would be difficulties with this because many functions are **cross-wired**, for example the right hand is controlled by the left hemisphere. Other functions, such as language, are **lateralised**.

Hemisphere deconnection

Hemisphere deconnection (also called the **split-brain operation**) involves cutting through the connections between the two hemispheres. One purpose for such an operation is to alleviate the symptoms of severe epilepsy. Epilepsy is a condition where the brain experiences a severe electrical storm. The neurons of the brain generate electrical currents to transmit their messages. In epilepsy some neurons discharge electrical signals inappropriately creating a 'storm'. In cases of severe epilepsy this storm is not confined to one area of the brain but spreads from hemisphere to hemisphere, magnifying the storm. This can be alleviated by deconnecting the hemispheres.

Studies of split-brain surgery have produced contradictory results. Animal operations have resulted in numerous behavioural effects whereas research with humans has shown no important behavioural effects.

Where does it all go wrong?

There's a lot of left and right to get right in this study.

L *is for* **L**eft *and for* **L**anguage

LVF *= left visual field*

This is found in both the left and right eye.

LVF of left eye goes to RIGHT hemisphere.

LVF of right eye goes to RIGHT hemisphere.

(RVF of both eyes goes to LEFT hemisphere.)

Left hand controlled by right hemisphere

Procedure

The apparatus used for testing

1   The participant has one eye covered and is asked to gaze at a fixed point in the centre of a projection screen.
2   Visual stimuli are back-projected onto the screen at a very high speed – one picture every 0.01 second or less. This means that the eye only has time to process the image in the visual field where it is placed.
3   Below the screen there is a gap so that participants can reach objects but not see what their hands are doing.

Testing participants

4   Participants are seated in front of the screen and asked to focus on a cross in the middle of the screen.
5   Images are shown on the left and right of the screen. Either one stimulus is flashed to one visual field or two stimuli are shown simultaneously – one to the right visual field (RVF) and one to the left visual field (LVF).
6   Participants asked to identify what is on the screen:
    • Say what they see: uses left hemisphere (LH), connected to the right visual field (RVF).
    • Spell out what they see: left hand controlled by right hemisphere (RH), related to left visual field (LVF).
    • Select an object from below the screen to match what they see (as above).
7   Dual-processing task – two objects are placed simultaneously one in each hand and then hidden in a pile of objects. Each hand is required to recognise the objects.
8   Participants **interviewed** about everyday effects.

Sample

The participants were a group of about 10 split-brain patients who suffered from severe epileptic seizures. They had the split-brain operation because their seizures could not be controlled by medication.

This was an **opportunity sample** of patients referred to the White Memorial Centre in Los Angeles, USA.

For most patients the operation reduced the frequency and severity of their seizures.

(+)　Enables the study of a rare condition.
(−)　The capabilities of epileptic patients may have been affected by their epileptic fits rather than just the split-brain operation, therefore findings are not generalisable.

Research method/technique

A **controlled observation** of split-brain patients to investigate behavioural symptoms resulting from hemisphere deconnection, a **snapshot** study.

This is also a **quasi-experiment**.

IV = Presence or absence of split-brain

DV = The participant's performance on various tasks

Hypothesis = Split-brain patients perform differently to individuals without a split-brain.

(+)　The use of objective tests to measure the patients' capabilities provides an unbiased means of assessing the effects of the operation.
(−)　In a quasi-experiment the IV has not been manipulated, nor are participants **randomly allocated** to conditions and therefore causal conclusions are not justified.

Qualitative data e.g. how a patient responded to a symbol displayed to RVF.
(+)　Allows researcher to gather rich, in-depth detail about the effects of the split-brain operation.
(−)　Not possible to apply statistics to the data, and consider the extent to which 'normal' and split-brain patients are different.

Findings

Display to left and right visual field – LVF and RVF

* If a $ sign is shown to LVF and ? sign to RVF, participant can draw $ sign with left hand (shows LVF is linked to left hand and therefore both linked to RH).
* Patient reports he saw the ? sign (shows RVF linked to LH where the language centres reside).

Visual material to RVF only

* Participant can describe visual material in speech and writing as normal (RVF linked to LH).

Visual material to LVF only

* Participant reports he saw nothing or saw a flash of light on left.
* Participant can select objects that are similar with left hand, e.g. select a wristwatch when shown a clock. Shows some language comprehension in RH.

Pinup to LVF

* Participant giggles but says he saw nothing.

Dual processing task

* Participant's right (or left) hand selects object presented to it, but each hand ignores the other hand's objects.

Everyday life

* Participants continue to watch TV or read books with no complaints; intellect and personality are unchanged. However, they have short term memory deficits and difficulties with concentration.

Describe how the physiological approach could explain the difficulties experienced by individuals with a 'split-brain'

The physiological approach explains underlying behaviour in terms of processes in the body and the brain. Therefore it could explain the difficulties experienced by individuals with a 'split-brain' in terms of the connection between the two hemispheres of the brain. As a result of having their corpus callosum severed, the two hemispheres of the brain work independently.

Sperry demonstrated how split-brain patients' brains function differently to a 'normal' brain. In split-brain patients information is not communicated from one side to the other, so, for example, if an object was presented to the left visual field (registered by the right hemisphere of 'split-brain' patients), they were unable to name what they had seen because speech is controlled by the left hemisphere. A 'normal' person would have no difficulty naming the object because the connection between right and left hemisphere permits the transfer of information.

Section A type questions

In Section A of the G542 exam there will always be one question worth 4 marks on the study by Sperry (split-brain).

The questions below give you a taste of the kinds of questions you will be expected to answer on this section of the exam. In the exam each question would specifically mention Sperry (split-brain).

1   The study by Sperry investigated the effects of hemisphere deconnection in split-brain patients.
    (a)   Describe what is meant by the term 'hemisphere deconnection'. **[2]**
    (b)   Identify **one** way hemisphere deconnection affected the participants when they were shown stimuli to one visual field. **[2]**

2   Describe **two** methods used to assess the abilities of split-brain patients. **[4]**

3   (a)   Identify **one** difference between 'split-brain' patients and 'normal' people in their ability to identify objects by touch alone. **[2]**
    (b)   Outline **one** reason for this difference. **[2]**

4   Describe how visual stimuli were presented to participants in this study. **[4]**

5   Outline **two** findings from Sperry's study on hemisphere deconnection. **[4]**

6   (a)   Give **one** reason why the participants had undergone an operation to deconnect the two hemispheres of the brain. **[2]**
    (b)   Describe how patients responded when an object was placed, out of sight, in their left hand. **[2]**

7   (a)   Describe how split-brain patients responded to visual material presented to their right visual field (RVF). **[2]**
    (b)   Outline **one** other finding from this study. **[2]**

8   (a)   Explain why a 'split-brain' patient could not describe in speech, material presented to their left visual field. **[2]**
    (b)   Explain why patients did not experience the same difficulties in their everyday lives. **[2]**

9   (a)   Describe the sample used in this study. **[2]**
    (b)   Outline **one** problem with generalising from the sample used in this study. **[2]**

10 (a)   Describe how split-brain patients responded to visual material presented to their left visual field (LVF). **[2]**
    (b)   Outline **one** conclusion that can be drawn from this finding. **[2]**

11 Sperry said, 'one hemisphere does not know what the other hemisphere has been doing'.
    (a)   Give **one** piece of evidence to support this statement. **[2]**
    (b)   Give **one** piece of evidence that challenges this statement. **[2]**

12 The right hemisphere has been called the 'silent hemisphere'.
    (a)   Give **one** piece of evidence to support this claim. **[2]**
    (b)   Identify **one** function that is controlled by the right hemisphere. **[2]**

13 (a)   Give **one** reason why the data may not be considered to be reliable. **[2]**
    (b)   Give **one** reason why the data may not be considered to be valid. **[2]**

14 (a)   Identify **two** behaviours controlled by the left hemisphere. **[2]**
    (b)   Give **one** piece of evidence that demonstrates your claim. **[2]**

15 (a)   Identify the independent variable (IV) in this study. **[2]**
    (b)   Explain why this independent variable (IV) could not be manipulated. **[2]**

16 (a)   Outline **one** way in which the sample may be considered representative. **[2]**
    (b)   Outline **one** way in which the sample may be considered unrepresentative. **[2]**

17 This study demonstrates that each side of the brain has different functions (called 'lateralisation').
    (a)   Identify **one** function exclusive to each side of the brain. **[2]**
    (b)   Explain why this lateralisation might cause a problem for some people. **[2]**

18 Sperry said that he was 'impressed by the patients' individual differences'.
    (a)   Explain what he meant by this. **[2]**
    (b)   Give **one** piece of evidence to support this statement. **[2]**

19 (a)   Identify **two** structures that were severed in the split-brain operation. **[2]**
    (b)   Explain why normal patients can say what they see in their left visual field. **[2]**

20 (a)   Describe **one** way in which the study lacked ecological validity. **[2]**
    (b)   Explain why it was appropriate for this study to lack ecological validity. **[2]**

See www.psypress.com/books/ details/9781848721807/ for suggested answers.

Section B type questions

In Section B of the G542 exam you will be asked to provide detailed information about one core study. The questions will be similar to those below. You should practise answering these questions in relation to the study by Sperry (split-brain).

Background and aims

1   Outline previous research related to the study by Sperry. [3]
2   What was the aim of the study by Sperry? [2]
3   State one hypothesis investigated in this study. [2]

Design and procedure

4   Explain why this study can be considered to be a quasi-experiment. [4]
5   Suggest one strength of using this method in the context of this study. [3]
6   Suggest one weakness of using this method in the context of this study. [3]
7   Describe the sample used in this study. [3]
8   Explain how the sample in this study was selected. [3]
9   Suggest one strength of using this sample. [3]
10 Suggest one weakness of using this sample. [3]
11 Explain why this study can be considered a snapshot study. [4]
12 With reference to this study, suggest one strength of conducting snapshot studies. [3]
13 With reference to this study, suggest one weakness of conducting snapshot studies. [3]
14 Describe two ethical issues raised by this study. [6]
15 Outline the procedure followed by this study. [8]
16 Describe improvements/changes that could be made to this study. [8]
17 Evaluate the improvements/changes that you have suggested. [8]

Findings

18 Give two examples of qualitative data that was collected in this study. [4]
19 Suggest one strength of the qualitative data collected. [3]
20 Suggest one weakness of the qualitative data collected. [3]
21 Outline the findings of this study. [8]
22 Discuss the reliability of the findings of this study. [6]
23 Discuss the validity of the conclusions of this study. [6]
24 Discuss the ecological validity of this study. [6]

> **Example answer for question 12**
>
> *Snapshot studies allow the researcher to compare individuals at one period in time to see how they may be similar or different.*
>
> **LINK TO STUDY...**
>
> *Sperry compared the test results of a group of nine split-brain patients to observe what capabilities they had in common. Such common traits could be attributed to the effects of hemisphere deconnection. The observations were made over a relatively short period of time. Patients' brains might develop compensations over time to deal with the operation if observed over a longer period of time.*

> **Exam advice question 15**
>
> - *The amount of detail is what matters. Include specific pieces of information of what was actually done.*
> - *Don't include any information on findings or aims.*

> **Example answer for question 21**
>
> *Don't forget that 'findings' and 'results' are the same thing, but 'findings' and 'conclusions' are not the same.*
>
> *A finding is a fact, it is evidence that has been provided. A conclusion is an interpretation of the facts.*
>
> *Stick to the facts when answering questions on findings/results.*

Section C type questions

In Section C of the G542 exam there is one question (four parts) on the approaches/perspectives.

1   Outline one assumption of the physiological approach. [2]
2   Describe how the physiological approach could explain the difficulties experienced by individuals with a split-brain. [4]
3   Describe one similarity and one difference between the study by Sperry and any other study that has followed the physiological approach. [6]
4   Discuss strengths and weaknesses of the physiological approach using examples from the Sperry study. [12]

> **Exam advice for question 4**
>
> *Strengths and weakness of the study will not be creditworthy – the focus is on the approach, using examples drawn from core studies.*

Milgram

Aim

The aim of this study is to investigate the process of obedience; to demonstrate the power of a **legitimate** authority even when a command requires destructive behaviour.

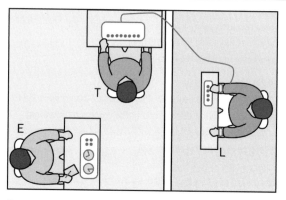

The set-up showing where each person was seated.

Context

Obedience

Obedience may be deeply ingrained in the human character and may be thought to be destructive, but we should also remember that it serves productive functions as well, such as acts of charity and kindness. Obedience is an indispensable part of social life. In order for people to live in communities some system of authority is required.

The 'Germans are different' hypothesis

The issue of obedience was particularly relevant after the Second World War, when explanations were sought for the inhumane obedience of Germans who systematically slaughtered millions of innocent people during the Second World War.

Milgram outlined his views in a film he made. He believed that the inhumane obedience of Nazi Germans could be explained by the fact that Germans are by disposition much more obedient than people from other cultures/countries; it is in their national character. Milgram intended to conduct this study with Germans but first wanted to run a **pilot study**, to see if his procedure worked. He did not expect high levels of obedience from Americans.

Where does it all go wrong?

It isn't an experiment.

Milgram called it an experiment but researchers are more careful now about what is and what isn't an experiment.

An experiment has to have an IV. The changing levels of shock are not IVs because they did not cause obedience – they were DVs because they measured how obedient a participant was.

The study was conducted in a laboratory and was highly controlled.

Extra tip: The participants were volunteers. Does that make them more or less likely to go along with the experimenter? There are arguments for either view.

Procedure

1   The study took place in a **laboratory** at Yale University, a prestigious institution.
2   Each participant was told that the study aimed to see how punishment affected learning (i.e. the true aim of the study was withheld). They were told they would receive $4.50 for participating and the money was theirs no matter what happened after they arrived.
3   The naïve volunteer participant was introduced to the other 'participant' (the accountant) and then lots were drawn for the parts of teacher and learner. The naïve 'true' participant always got the part of teacher.
4   Learner and teacher were taken to the laboratory where the learner was strapped into an 'electric chair apparatus' in order to prevent excessive movement when the electric shocks were delivered. An electrode was attached to the learner's wrist and connected to a shock generator in the next room. The experimenter advised them that no tissue damage would be caused by the shocks, although they would be painful. The teacher experienced a test shock of 45 volts.
5   The teacher (T) read questions out to the learner (L) who sat in a separate room in front of a four-way panel to select answers (see diagram above).
6   If the teacher expressed a desire to stop delivering shocks, then the experimenter (E) had a set of statements ('prods') to deliver, e.g. *The experiment requires that you continue*, and *You have no choice, you must continue*.
7   When the shock level reached 300 volts the learner had been instructed to bang on the wall. After that he stopped responding.
8   Participants were **debriefed** after the study.

Sample

Milgram placed an advert in a local paper and also sent out a mailshot in the post. Participants were sought for a scientific study related to memory. They must be men between the ages of 20 and 50 and not high school or college students.

A final group of 40 participants were selected from the 500 who volunteered, consisting of 40 men from various occupational and educational backgrounds. It is a **self-selected sample**.

A biology teacher, dressed in a technician's coat, played the part of the experimenter. The learner (or victim) was played by a 47-year-old accountant, trained for the role. Both of these men were accomplices of Milgram (i.e. they were **confederates**).

(+) Sample included men from a range of occupations and educational backgrounds so was likely to be representative of the **target population**, so findings in relation to obedience were generalisable.

(–) Cannot generalise to all people on the basis of an all male sample and all American.

Research method/technique

This is a **controlled observation** (in a **laboratory**) using **self-report**.

It is not an experiment because there was no **independent variable** (see explanation on facing page).

(+) Observation can capture spontaneous and unexpected behaviour, and produce 'rich' qualitative and/or quantitative data.

(–) Participants may respond differently in a laboratory environment than they would in everyday life. They may have just 'gone along' with the researcher to help this important scientific research.

Findings

Quantitative data

- All 40 participants (100%) continued giving shocks up to 300 volts.
- Five participants (12.5%) stopped at this critical point of 300 volts.
- Nine more participants stopped between 315 and 375 volts (four stopped at 315 volts, two at 330 volts, one at 345 volts, one at 360 volts and one at 375 volts).
- 26 out of 40 participants (65%) continued to the end (450 volts) and were considered obedient.
- 14 out of 40 participants were therefore considered disobedient.

Qualitative data

- Many participants showed signs of nervousness.
- Participants were observed to sweat, tremble, stutter, bite their lips, groan and dig their fingernails into their flesh.
- Full-blown uncontrollable seizures were observed for three participants, in one case so violent that the trial had to be stopped.
- Participants' comments showed their distress, e.g. *He's banging in there. I'm gonna chicken out. I'd like to continue, but I can't do that to a man … I'm sorry I can't do that to a man. I'll hurt his heart. You take your [money].*

Quantitative data e.g. number of participants who fully obeyed.

(+) Provides direct means of assessing levels of obedience, enabling simple conclusions to be drawn.

(–) Provides oversimplified explanation of a complex behaviour.

Qualitative data e.g. observations of behaviour.

(+) Provides rich, in-depth detail about a complex behaviour.

(–) Makes it difficult to draw simple conclusions about why people obey.

Describe how the social approach could explain obedience

The social approach explains <u>behaviour</u> in terms of the people around us and the interactions between us. Therefore obedience could be explained in terms of the way other people are behaving around us.

Milgram suggested that the presence of what appeared to be a legitimate authority figure, dressed in a white laboratory coat, carrying a clip board, influenced the participants' behaviour as they believed him to be a trustworthy and knowledgeable individual who should be obeyed.

Describe how the behaviourist perspective could explain obedience

The behaviourist perspective explains <u>behaviour</u> in terms of learning through direct experience (**classical** and **operant conditioning**) or indirect rewards (**social learning**). Therefore it could explain obedience in terms of these processes. For example, individuals may learn that obedience is rewarded by observing the behaviour of others who act as **role models**.

Section A type questions

In Section A of the G542 exam there will always be one question worth 4 marks on the study by Milgram (obedience).

The questions below give you a taste of the kinds of questions you will be expected to answer on this section of the exam. In the exam each question would specifically mention Milgram (obedience).

1   (a)   Describe the sample used in this study. **[2]**
    (b)   Outline **one** weakness of this sample. **[2]**

2   (a)   Describe **one** ethical issue in this study. **[2]**
    (b)   Describe what steps Milgram took to deal with this ethical issue. **[2]**

3   (a)   Describe **one** finding from this study. **[2]**
    (b)   State **one** conclusion that can be drawn from this finding. **[2]**

4   Outline **two** features of the Milgram study of obedience that made it seem real to the participants. **[4]**

5   (a)   Outline **one** way in which the sample may be considered representative. **[2]**
    (b)   Outline **one** way in which the sample may be considered unrepresentative. **[2]**

6   (a)   Describe how obedience was measured. **[2]**
    (b)   Suggest **one** problem with measuring obedience in this way. **[2]**

7   One ethical issue in psychological research is the 'right to withdraw'.
    (a)   Explain what steps Milgram took to ensure that participants had the right to withdraw. **[2]**
    (b)   Explain what aspects of the study meant they may not have felt they had the right to withdraw. **[2]**

8   (a)   Describe how the sample in this study was obtained. **[2]**
    (b)   Outline **one** advantage of the way this sample was obtained. **[2]**

9   Milgram, in his study of obedience, offered several suggestions for why participants (the teachers) obeyed. Describe **two** of these suggestions. **[4]**

10 Milgram found that all participants continued to deliver shocks until the point when the learner pounded on the wall.
    (a)   Give **one** conclusion that can be drawn from this finding. **[2]**
    (b)   Outline Milgram's reason for doing this research. **[2]**

11 Milgram instructed the experimenter to deliver four 'prods' if a participant expressed a wish to stop. Give **two** of these prods. **[4]**

12 (a)   Identify **two** findings from this study. **[2]**
    (b)   Outline **one** explanation Milgram gave for his findings. **[2]**

13 This study involved two confederates playing the role of learner and experimenter. Describe these **two** confederates. **[4]**

14 (a)   What did the participants believe was the aim of the study? **[2]**
    (b)   Describe the true aim of the study. **[2]**

15 (a)   Give **one** reason why the data may be considered to be reliable. **[2]**
    (b)   Explain why reliability is important. **[2]**

16 (a)   Identify **two** controls used in this study. **[2]**
    (b)   Explain why it was important to use controls in this study. **[2]**

17 It was important that participants believed the 'set-up'. Identify **two** procedures used to ensure that participants believed the learner was receiving shocks. **[4]**

18 Milgram claimed that extraordinary tension was generated by the procedures. Outline **two** pieces of evidence from the study that supports this suggestion. **[4]**

19 Outline **two** ways in which this study can be said to be low in ecological validity. **[4]**

20 (a)   Outline **two** ways that the procedures were standardised. **[2]**
    (b)   Explain why it was necessary to standardise procedures. **[2]**

See www.psypress.com/
books/details/9781848721807/
for suggested answers.

Section B type questions

In Section B of the G542 exam you will be asked to provide detailed information about one core study. The questions will be similar to those below. You should practise answering these questions in relation to the study by Milgram (obedience).

Background and aims

1   Outline previous research related to the study by Milgram. **[3]**

2   What was the aim of the study by Milgram? **[2]**

Design and procedure

3   Explain why this study can be considered to be a controlled observation. **[4]**

4   Suggest **one** strength of using this method in the context of this study. **[3]**

5   Suggest **one** weakness of using this method in the context of this study. **[3]**

6   Describe the sample used in this study. **[3]**

7   Explain how the sample in this study was selected. **[3]**

8   Suggest **one** strength of using this sample. **[3]**

9   Suggest **one** weakness of using this sample. **[3]**

10 Describe **two** ethical issues raised by this study. **[6]**

11 Outline the procedure followed by this study. **[8]**

12 Describe improvements/changes that could be made to this study. **[8]**

13 Evaluate the improvements/changes that you have suggested. **[8]**

Findings

14 Give **two** examples of quantitative data that was collected in this study. **[4]**

15 Suggest **one** strength of the quantitative data collected. **[3]**

16 Suggest **one** weakness of the quantitative data collected. **[3]**

17 Give **two** examples of qualitative data that was collected in this study. **[4]**

18 Suggest **one** strength of the qualitative data collected. **[3]**

19 Suggest **one** weakness of the qualitative data collected. **[3]**

20 Outline the findings of this study. **[8]**

21 Discuss the reliability of the findings of this study. **[6]**

22 Discuss the validity of the conclusions of this study. **[6]**

23 Discuss the ecological validity of this study. **[6]**

Exam advice on question 7

There is a distinction between question 6, where you are required to describe the sample, and question 7, where the focus must be on how it was selected.

There were three important aspects of 'how':

1 *There was an advertisement in local newspaper asking for volunteers (only males, not students).*

2 *A direct mailshot was used sending the advertisement out by post.*

3 *A final selection of 40 was made from the 500 who had applied to provide a variety of occupations and educations.*

Exam advice for question 12

Detail is so important for getting high marks, as the example above shows. It's not just about providing an answer but adding detail to your answer.

That is especially important in a question worth 8 marks. Just writing a list of improvements/changes will not attract high marks. Select a few improvements/changes and then provide specific details of what you would do. That's where the hard work – and the marks – comes in.

Exam advice for question 20

This question requires you to report the findings of this study – sometimes the term 'results' is used but they mean the same thing.

However, 'findings' and 'conclusions' are different. A finding is a fact, it is evidence that has been provided. A conclusion is an interpretation of the facts.

Stick to the facts when answering questions on findings/results.

Section C type questions

In Section C of the G542 exam there is one question (four parts) on the approaches/perspectives.

1   Outline **one** assumption of the social approach. **[2]**

2   Describe how the social approach could explain obedience. **[4]**

3   Describe **one** similarity and **one** difference between the study by Milgram and any other study that has followed the social approach. **[6]**

4   Discuss strengths and weaknesses of the social approach using examples from the Milgram study. **[12]**

You should answer these questions in relation to the behaviourist perspective and psychodynamic perspective as well.

Reicher and Haslam

Context

Understanding tyranny

Tyranny is defined by Reicher and Haslam as *an unequal social system involving the arbitrary or oppressive use of power by one group or its agents over another*.

Psychologists have explained tyranny (anti-social behaviour) in terms of group processes. For example, Gustav LeBon argued that individuals lose their sense of personal identity and responsibility when in a crowd and thus become capable of barbaric acts. This is called **deindividuation**.

Stanford Prison Experiment

Philip Zimbardo supported this deindividuation explanation in the Stanford Prison Experiment (SPE). Twenty-four participants were **randomly allocated** to the role of prisoner or guard. The study showed that immersion in a group (being in the prisoner group or the guard group) undermined the constraints that normally prevent anti-social behaviour. In addition, when a group has power, this seems to encourage extreme anti-social behaviour.

A different explanation

Reicher and Haslam offer a different explanation for anti-social group behaviour. **Social identity theory** suggests that individuals behave in an anti-social manner because they identify with a group that has anti-social norms.

Tyranny exists because there are group inequalities – some groups are dominant whereas others are subordinate. People prefer to belong to dominant groups because such groups have power and group membership enhances their own identity. Members of subordinate groups feel powerless and unable to challenge dominant groups.

An example of tyranny: German concentration camp.

Aim

The aim of this study is to:

- Study the interactions between dominant and subordinate groups.
- Understand the conditions under which subordinate groups will challenge the inequalities between dominant and subordinate groups, and thus overthrow tyranny.
- Investigate the conditions under which people identify with their groups.

Where does it all go wrong?

Get to grips with the IVs and how each affected behaviour.

IV	Low	High
Permeability	Identify with group, challenge inequality	Less identification, feel content with status quo
Legitimacy		
Cognitive alternatives		Create insecurity, challenge inequality

Procedure

1   The BBC built a simulated prison environment at Elstree Studios in London, and filmed and broadcast the study.
2   The 15 participants were divided into five groups of three where the members of each group were **matched** in terms of racism, **authoritarianism** and social dominance, for example. One member of each group was **randomly** selected to be a guard (N=5) and the rest were prisoners (N=10).
3   The guards were briefed the night before the study began. They were told to draw up the rules of the institution and told they must respect the basic rights of the prisoners. The guards had far better accommodation and food than the prisoners, creating a sense of inequality.
4   The prisoners arrived one at a time. Their heads were shaved and they were given numbered orange uniforms.
5   Throughout the study participants were regularly asked to rate themselves on e.g. social identification and authoritarianism (the DVs). Records of conversations were kept. Swabs of saliva were taken to assess stress levels.
6   **Permeability intervention**: The prisoners believed the guards had been selected because of certain personality characteristics but that if they showed similar traits they might be promoted to being a guard, creating permeability. On day 3 one prisoner was promoted but after that they were told no more promotions were possible, creating impermeability.
7   **Legitimacy intervention**: Participants were to be told that roles had been **randomly allocated**, i.e. the groups were not legitimate, creating insecurity and a search for cognitive alternatives. (In fact this was not needed because the ineffective leadership meant insecurity was created.)
8   **Cognitive alternatives**: Prisoner 10 (trade unionist) was introduced on day 5 to provide cognitive alternatives. This would challenge inequality and create insecurity.

Sample

Male volunteers were sought through national newspapers and leaflets (a **self-selected sample**). An initial pool of 332 applicants was reduced to 27 through screening that involved psychological and medical screening.

The final 15 male participants were selected to represent diverse social and ethnic backgrounds.

Ⓔ

(+) A wide range of social and ethnic backgrounds means that the sample is representative of the **target population**, making the findings generalisable.

(−) Cannot generalise to all people on the basis of an all male sample and all British.

Research method/technique

This is a **controlled observation** involving **role play** and **self-report**. It could also be regarded as an **experimental case study**.

The use of planned interventions means that it can also be regarded as a **field experiment**.

IVs = Permeability, legitimacy, cognitive alternatives

DVs = Social (e.g. social identification), organisational (e.g. compliance with rules), clinical (e.g. depression)

Hypotheses = Members of dominant groups seek no change when group identity is strong.

Members of subordinate groups identify with their group (and challenge inequality) when permeability is low and legitimacy/security is low.

Ⓔ

(+) The manipulation of key variables (e.g. permeability) allows causal conclusions to be drawn.

(−) Participants were aware that their behaviour was being filmed and may not have acted as they would if it were a real situation.

Findings

Phase 1: Rejecting inequality

- Prisoners initially showed little social identification. Once boundaries became impermeable (promotion on day 3) social identification ratings increased and this was reflected in prisoners' conversations (e.g. they discussed how they could change the system).
- The guards, unexpectedly, showed little social identification, which led to ineffective leadership.
- Ineffective leadership meant that the prisoners no longer perceived the inequalities as legitimate (the guards did not deserve their privileges), creating insecurity.
- The introduction of prisoner 10 did lead to increasing awareness of cognitive alternatives, as measured by **rating scales**.
- Measures of organisational variables dropped **significantly** on day 5 when the prisoners started to challenge the guards and no longer supported the organisation.
- On day 6 there was a collapse of the prisoner–guard system.

Phase 2: Embracing inequality

- Participants set up an egalitarian social system which soon failed.
- The suggested replacement was a tyrannical regime, reflected in a rise in right-wing authoritarianism (as measured by rating scales).
- The new regime was judged not **ethical** and therefore the study was stopped after eight days.

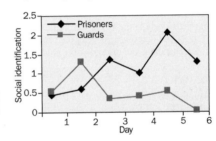

Graph showing changes in social identification.

Ⓔ

Quantitative data e.g. social identification scores.

(+) Provides simple means of seeing behavioural changes.

(−) Oversimplifies people's thoughts and feelings.

Qualitative data e.g. conversations between prisoners.

(+) Rich, in-depth detail about factors that cause tyranny.

(−) Often unique data, making analysis of prisoners'/ guards' attitudes difficult.

Describe how the social approach could explain tyranny

The social approach explains behaviour In terms of the people around us and the interactions between us. Therefore it could explain tyranny in terms of dominant and subordinate groups.

Reicher and Haslam found that subordinate groups will challenge the inequalities between dominant and subordinate groups when they identify with their group and when permeability is low and legitimacy is low.

Section A type questions

In Section A of the G542 exam there will always be one question worth 4 marks on the study by Reicher and Haslam (BBC prison study).

The questions below give you a taste of the kinds of questions you will be expected to answer on this section of the exam. In the exam each question would specifically mention Reicher and Haslam (BBC prison study).

1 (a) Outline why the study may be considered an experiment. **[2]**
   (b) Outline why the study may be considered a case study. **[2]**

2 There were three independent variables (IVs) in this study. Describe **two** of these IVs. **[4]**

3 (a) Describe what is meant by the term 'tyranny'. **[2]**
   (b) Describe **one** way to create a situation in which tyranny could develop. **[2]**

4 Describe how the sample was recruited in this study. **[4]**

5 Outline **one** piece of evidence from the study that supports the suggestion that group processes can create tyranny. **[4]**

6 (a) Identify **one** difference between the guards at the beginning and the end of the study. **[2]**
   (b) Identify **one** difference between the prisoners at the beginning and the end of the study. **[2]**

7 Outline **two** reasons why the prisoners were given uniforms. **[4]**

8 (a) Identify **two** dependent variables (DVs) in this study. **[2]**
   (b) Describe how **one** of these dependent variables (DVs) was measured. **[2]**

9 (a) Describe **one** way the researchers tried to ensure ethical guidelines were upheld. **[2]**
   (b) Outline **one** reason why stress or psychological harm is an ethical concern in this study. **[2]**

10 (a) Describe how 'permeability' was created. **[2]**
   (b) Outline how the behaviour of the prisoners changed once the groups became impermeable. **[2]**

11 (a) Select **one** independent variable (IV) and **one** dependent variable (DV) and explain the effect of this IV on the DV. **[2]**
   (b) Outline **one** conclusion that can be drawn from this finding. **[2]**

12 Describe the screening process that reduced the initial pool of 332 applicants to 27 participants. **[4]**

13 (a) Describe how legitimacy was planned to be created. **[2]**
   (b) Explain why this intervention was not necessary. **[2]**

14 (a) Explain why the study ended prematurely. **[2]**
   (b) Give **one** conclusion that can be drawn from this study. **[2]**

15 The group of 15 participants were divided into groups of three that were matched.
   (a) Identify **two** criteria used for matching. **[2]**
   (b) Explain why it is necessary to match participants in this way. **[2]**

16 (a) Describe how 'cognitive alternatives' were created. **[2]**
   (b) Outline how the behaviour of the prisoners changed once the prisoners were exposed to a cognitive alternative. **[2]**

17 Describe the prison environment created for this study. **[4]**

18 (a) Describe how **one** of the dependent variables (DVs) was measured in this study. **[2]**
   (b) Explain how the reliability of this measurement could have been assessed. **[2]**

19 (a) Explain what is meant by 'permeability'. **[2]**
   (b) Outline **one** way that permeability was changed. **[2]**

20 (a) Outline **one** way in which the sample may be considered representative. **[2]**
   (b) Outline **one** way in which the sample may be considered unrepresentative. **[2]**

See www.psypress.com/
books/details/9781848721807/
for suggested answers.

Section B type questions

In Section B of the G542 exam you will be asked to provide detailed information about one core study. The questions will be similar to those below. You should practise answering these questions in relation to the study by Reicher and Haslam (BBC prison study).

Background and aims

1. Outline previous research related to the study by Reicher and Haslam. **[3]**
2. What was the aim of the study by Reicher and Haslam? **[2]**
3. State **one** hypothesis investigated in this study. **[2]**

> **Exam advice for question 2**
>
> *The aim of a study is not the same as a hypothesis, though often they overlap.*

Design and procedure

4. Explain why this study can be considered to be a field experiment. **[4]**
5. Suggest **one** strength of using this method in the context of this study. **[3]**
6. Suggest **one** weakness of using this method in the context of this study. **[3]**
7. Describe the sample used in this study. **[3]**
8. Explain how the sample in this study was selected. **[3]**
9. Suggest **one** strength of using this sample. **[3]**
10. Suggest **one** weakness of using this sample. **[3]**
11. Explain why this study can be considered a longitudinal study. **[4]**
12. With reference to this study, suggest **one** strength of conducting longitudinal studies. **[3]**
13. With reference to this study, suggest **one** weakness of conducting longitudinal studies. **[3]**
14. Describe **two** ethical issues raised by this study. **[6]**
15. Outline the procedure followed by this study. **[8]**
16. Describe improvements/changes that could be made to this study. **[8]**
17. Evaluate the improvements/changes that you have suggested. **[8]**

> **Exam advice for questions 16 and 17**
>
> *Sometimes questions 16 and 17 are joined together so there are 4 marks for describing the improvements and four marks for evaluating them.*

> **Example answer for question 22**
>
> *In order to get the full 3 marks your answer must be detailed and must be linked to the study.*
>
> *For example:*
>
> > *Qualitative data allows the researcher to gather rich, in-depth detail about an individual or small organised group.*
>
> **LINK TO STUDY...**
>
> > *Reicher and Haslam were able to understand why prisoners wanted to change groups by asking questions that produced qualitative data.*
> >
> > *An example of this is that one prisoner said: 'I'd like to be a guard because they get all the luxuries and we do not.'*

Findings

18. Give **two** examples of quantitative data that was collected in this study. **[4]**
19. Suggest **one** strength of the data collected. **[3]**
20. Suggest **one** weakness of the data collected. **[3]**
21. Give **two** examples of qualitative data that was collected in this study. **[4]**
22. Suggest **one** strength of the data collected. **[3]**
23. Suggest **one** weakness of the data collected. **[3]**
24. Outline the findings of this study. **[8]**
25. Discuss the reliability of the findings of this study. **[6]**
26. Discuss the validity of the conclusions of this study. **[6]**
27. Discuss the ecological validity of this study. **[6]**

> **Exam advice for question 24**
>
> *Less is more*
>
> *You do need quite a few findings but you also must provide details, so it may be better to memorise fewer findings but know the details for each.*

Section C type questions

In Section C of the G542 exam there is one question (four parts) on the approaches/perspectives.

1. Outline **one** assumption of the social approach. **[2]**
2. Describe how the social approach could explain tyranny. **[4]**
3. Describe **one** similarity and **one** difference between the study by Reicher and Haslam and any other study that has followed the social approach. **[6]**
4. Discuss strengths and weaknesses of the social approach using examples from the Reicher and Haslam study. **[12]**

> **Exam advice on question 4**
>
> *In the actual exam you will be able to use any study that is relevant to the social approach, which includes the three social core studies (Milgram, Reicher and Haslam, and Piliavin et al.) as well as Bandura et al.*

Context

The murder of Kitty Genovese

A brutal murder in New York triggered psychologists' interest in **bystander behaviour**. A young woman, Kitty Genovese, was attacked and stabbed on her way home from work at 3 am. She screamed and at least 38 neighbours heard her. One shouted at the attacker, who ran away only to return later, fatally stabbing Kitty at the entrance to her apartment. It was reported that no one rang the police until after she had been murdered.

Bystander behaviour

Bystander behaviour refers to how bystanders behave in emergency situations, i.e. when someone requires help because of an accident. Research has indicated that people are actually less willing to help if there are other bystanders and more willing to help if they are the only bystander. This has led to the term 'bystander apathy', describing the reduced helpfulness of bystanders in large groups.

Diffusion of responsibility

Two psychologists, Darley and Latané, proposed an explanation based on their own research. They found that the more people there were, the less likely each individual was to ask, suggesting that this was because each person felt less responsibility. They coined the phrase '**diffusion of responsibility**' for this explanation.

However, their research was conducted in **laboratories** – which is not a problem if some research is also conducted in the field to provide confirmation of this behaviour in a more natural setting.

Where does it all go wrong?

Students often forget this is an experiment – they think it is just an observation. There are observational elements but there are also IVs and this makes it an experiment.

Students also include gender of victim as an IV – it isn't. The victims were always male.

Piliavin *et al.* included a proposed model of helping behaviour in emergency situations. Don't forget that arousal is part of this model: heightened arousal leads to a wish to reduce arousal. A decision is made about whether to help based on a cost–reward matrix:

	Help	Don't help
Costs	Effort	Blame
Rewards	Praise	Get on with activities

Aim

The aim of this study is to test the diffusion of responsibility hypothesis – group size is negatively related to willingness to help in an emergency situation.

The aim of the study is also to investigate the effect of certain variables on individuals' willingness to help (**helping behaviour**):

- Type of victim (drunk or with a cane).
- Race of victim (black or white).
- Modelling – seeing someone else being helpful.

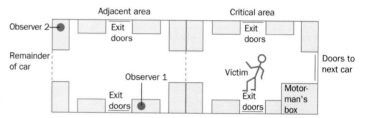

The layout of subway carriage showing the critical area and position of the victim.

Procedure

1. There were four teams of students from Columbia University (aged 24–35). Each team consisted of a male victim, male **model** and two female observers to record activity.
2. There were 103 trials. Each was one ride on the express subway lasting 7½ minutes (from one stop to the next).
3. On each trial the team of four students boarded a subway train using different doors, varying the location of the experimental car.
4. The victim always stood next to a pole in the centre of the critical area. After 70 seconds the victim staged a collapse and remained on the floor until help was forthcoming or until the train stopped, when the model helped him up.
5. On 38 trials the victim smelled of alcohol and carried a bottle wrapped tightly in a brown bag (drunk condition), while on the remaining 65 trials he appeared sober and carried a black cane (cane condition). In all other aspects victims dressed and behaved identically in both conditions.
6. There were four model conditions: the model stood in the critical or adjacent area and was either helped early (70 seconds after initial collapse) or late (150 seconds later).
7. The observers sat outside the critical area and recorded data as unobtrusively as possible during the ride.
   - One noted the race, sex and location (RSL) of people in the critical area, counted the people in the car and the number of people who helped plus their RSL.
   - A second observer noted the RSL of people in the adjacent area, and noted how long it took for the first person to help after the victim collapsed and/or after the model appeared.
   - Both observers recorded comments spontaneously made by nearby passengers and attempted to elicit comments from a rider sitting next to them.

Sample

The participants in this study were an **opportunity sample** of passengers on the New York subway during the middle of the day (11 am to 3 pm) through the period from 15 April to 26 June 1968.

In total there were about 4,450 men and women passengers on the trains. The racial composition of a typical train was about 45% black and 55% white. The **mean** number of people per car during these hours was 43, the mean number of people in the 'critical area', in which the incident took place, was 8.5.

Confederates played the role of victim and models.

(+) A very large sample which should be representative of the **target population**.

(–) Sample was drawn from the New York area, so results cannot be generalised to individuals from other non-urban areas/countries whose helping behaviour may be different.

Research method/technique

This is a **field experiment** with **independent measures** and using **observational techniques**, a **snapshot** study.

IV = Type of victim (drunk or cane), race (black or white), presence of model, group size

DV = Time it took for help to be offered, number of people who offered help

Hypothesis e.g. People give help more quickly if a victim is white rather than black. (Other hypotheses were developed from the aims.)

(+) Conducting the study in a natural environment shows helping behaviour in people's everyday lives.

(–) Many variables were not controlled, such as people being distracted by the pressures of urban life.

Findings

The frequency of helping was considerably higher than found in **laboratory experiments**.

Drunk or using cane

- An apparently disabled person (using a cane) is more likely to receive help than one who appears drunk (95% versus 50%).
- Help is forthcoming more quickly for a disabled person: 87% of the 'disabled' victims were helped before the model acted, whereas only 17% of the drunk victims were helped.
- The **median** latency for cane trials (non-model condition) was 5 seconds; it was 109 seconds for drunk trials.

Race and gender

- Black victims received help less quickly than white victims.
- There was a slight 'same race effect' in the drunk condition (people more likely to be helped by someone of the same race).
- 90% of first helpers were male, whereas only 60% of passengers were male.

Modelling

- The model intervening early (after 70 seconds) had slightly more effect than the late model (at 150 seconds). There was only a small amount of data on this as most victims were helped before a model could step in.

Group size

- 'Diffusion of responsibility' was not found in this study; helping was greater in seven-person than three-person groups.

Comments from passengers

- For example, *It's for men to help him* or *You feel so bad when you don't know what to do.*

Quantitative data e.g. number of people helping.

(+) Makes it easy to compare the behaviour towards drunk and 'disabled' confederates.

(–) Oversimplifies the factors that affect helping behaviour.

Qualitative data e.g. participants' comments.

(+) Provides in-depth insights about people's attitudes and thoughts.

(–) Difficult to analyse such data.

Describe how the social approach could explain helping behaviour

The social approach explains <u>behaviour</u> in terms of the people around us and the interactions between us. Therefore it could explain helping behaviour in terms of the behaviour of others and the social situation.

Piliavin *et al.* found that when models intervened to offer help this did encourage helping behaviour, though often this was not necessary. The social situation (a closed subway carriage with a clear emergency) led to a high rate of helping presumably because the costs of not helping were high and the costs of helping were low.

The characteristics of the victim were important (e.g. being drunk or not). The race of the victim was less important though there was a slight same-race effect.

Section A type questions

In Section A of the G542 exam there will always be one question worth 4 marks on the study by Piliavin, Rodin and Piliavin (subway Samaritan).

The questions below give you a taste of the kinds of questions you will be expected to answer on this section of the exam. In the exam each question would specifically mention Piliavin, Rodin and Piliavin (subway Samaritan).

1 (a) Identify **two** independent variables (IVs) in this experiment. **[2]**
   (b) Outline how **one** of these independent variables (IVs) was manipulated in this experiment. **[2]**

2 Describe how the individuals played the role of victim. **[4]**

3 Outline **two** ways in which this study can be said to be high in ecological validity. **[4]**

4 (a) Outline **two** ways that procedure was standardised. **[2]**
   (b) Explain why it is important to standardise procedures. **[2]**

5 Outline **two** practical problems that may have occurred in this study. **[4]**

6 (a) Give **one** example of the qualitative data that was gathered in this study. **[2]**
   (b) Give **one** strength of collecting qualitative data in this study. **[2]**

7 Describe the participants in this study. **[4]**

8 (a) Identify **one** of the model conditions. **[2]**
   (b) Outline **one** finding from the model conditions. **[2]**

9 The findings from this study are shown in the table below.

	Median latency for help to be forthcoming
Drunk	109 seconds
With cane	5 seconds

   (a) Explain what 'median latency' means. **[2]**
   (b) Outline **one** conclusion that can be drawn from this table. **[2]**

10 (a) Identify **two** controls used in this study. **[2]**
   (b) Explain why **one** of these controls was used. **[2]**

11 (a) Outline **one** ethical issue raised in this study. **[2]**
   (b) Explain how this ethical issue might have been dealt with. **[2]**

12 (a) Identify **two** dependent variables (DVs) in this study. **[2]**
   (b) Explain how **one** of these DVs was measured. **[2]**

13 (a) What is meant by the term 'diffusion of responsibility'? **[2]**
   (b) Outline **one** reason why diffusion of responsibility was not found in this study. **[2]**

14 Identify the **four** independent variables (IVs) in this study. **[4]**

15 Two student confederates sat outside the critical area. Describe what role they played in this study. **[4]**

16 (a) Describe how the participants responded to the drunk victim. **[2]**
   (b) Outline **one** conclusion that can be drawn from this evidence. **[2]**

17 The aim of this study was to investigate the effect of certain variables on individuals' willingness to help (helping behaviour).
   (a) Identify **one** of these variables. **[2]**
   (b) Outline **one** conclusion related to this variable. **[2]**

18 (a) Describe how helping behaviour was measured. **[2]**
   (b) Suggest **one** problem with measuring helping behaviour in this way. **[2]**

19 (a) Outline **one** way in which the sample may be considered representative. **[2]**
   (b) Outline **one** way in which the sample may be considered unrepresentative. **[2]**

20 Describe what happened on each trial of this study. **[4]**

See www.psypress.com/books/details/9781848721807/ for suggested answers.

Section B type questions

In Section B of the G542 exam you will be asked to provide detailed information about one core study. The questions will be similar to those below. You should practise answering these questions in relation to the study by Piliavin, Rodin and Piliavin (subway Samaritan).

Background and aims

1 Outline previous research related to the study by Piliavin *et al.* [3]

2 What was the aim of the study by Piliavin *et al.*? [2]

3 State the hypothesis investigated in this study. [2]

Design and procedure

4 Explain why this study can be considered to be a field experiment. [4]

5 Suggest **one** strength of using this method in the context of this study. [3]

6 Suggest **one** weakness of using this method in the context of this study. [3]

7 Describe the sample used in this study. [3]

8 Explain how the sample in this study was selected. [3]

9 Suggest **one** strength of using this sample. [3]

10 Suggest **one** weakness of using this sample. [3]

11 Explain why this study can be considered a snapshot study. [4]

12 With reference to this study, suggest **one** strength of conducting snapshot studies. [3]

13 With reference to this study, suggest **one** weakness of conducting snapshot studies. [3]

14 Describe **two** ethical issues raised by this study. [6]

15 Outline the procedure followed by this study. [8]

16 Suggest how the procedure followed in this study could be improved. [8]

17 Outline the implications of the procedural changes you have suggested for this study. [8]

Findings

18 Give **two** examples of quantitative data that was collected in this study. [4]

19 Suggest **one** strength of the quantitative data collected. [3]

20 Suggest **one** weakness of the quantitative data collected. [3]

21 Outline the findings of this study. [8]

22 Discuss the reliability of the findings of this study. [6]

23 Discuss the validity of the conclusions of this study. [6]

24 Discuss the ecological validity of this study. [6]

Example answer for question 14

There are two obvious ethical issues: consent was not gained from participants and the participants were deceived.

However, just stating these issues is not enough for 6 marks. Elaboration is required.

For example:

The participants were deceived because they saw a person collapse on the subway and believed something was wrong. In fact the 'victim' was only acting. This is an ethical issue because participants might have felt quite upset by seeing someone like this, especially if this triggered something in their minds – like remembering a close friend being injured. Furthermore it is an issue because the participants were not debriefed, so they never knew that it was just acting.

A second ethical issue would need to be covered in the same way.

Exam advice on questions 16 and 17

This is a slight variation of the usual question that asks more generally about improvements/ changes. The focus is just on procedure – so sampling would not be creditworthy.

Section C type questions

In Section C of the G542 exam there is one question (four parts) on the approaches/perspectives.

1 Outline **one** assumption of the social approach. [2]

2 Describe how the social approach could explain helping behaviour. [4]

3 Describe **one** similarity and **one** difference between the study by Piliavin *et al.* and any other study that has followed the social approach. [6]

4 Discuss strengths and weaknesses of the social approach using examples from the Piliavin *et al.* study. [12]

Exam advice on questions 1 and 2

Answers in the exam must always include the word 'behaviour'.

Rosenhan

Context

The anti-psychiatry movement

In the 1960s, psychiatrists such as Michel Foucault, Ronnie Laing and Thomas Szasz launched the 'anti-psychiatry' movement, challenging the fundamental claims and practices of mainstream psychiatry. According to mainsteam psychiatry, mental illness is similar to physical illness and can be diagnosed by identifying symptoms and syndromes. The DSM (*Diagnostic and Statistical Manual of Mental Disorders*) is used for this purpose.

The anti-psychiatry movement proposed that the concepts of sanity and insanity are merely social constructs, i.e. they are not 'real' but are simply constructions made by a particular society.

Mental illness and the law

David Rosenhan had an interest in both psychology and the law, and noted that it was common to read about murder trials where the prosecution and defence each call their own psychiatrists who disagree on the defendant's sanity.

Such disputes led him to agree with the anti-psychiatry movement and ask *If sanity and insanity exist, how shall we know them?* We may be convinced that we can tell the normal from the **abnormal**, but the evidence for this ability is not quite as compelling as we think.

This is not to deny that there are deviant or odd behaviours – murder and hallucinations are deviant. Nor is it to deny that 'mental illness' does cause personal anguish – depression, for example, is linked to psychological suffering.

Once you become a patient in a psychiatric hospital, does everything you do provide evidence of your insanity – even if you are sane?

Aim

The aim of this study is to investigate whether a diagnosis of insanity is based on characteristics of patients themselves or, instead, on the context in which the patient is seen.

- To see if sane individuals would be diagnosed as insane just because they presented themselves to a psychiatric hospital claiming to have psychiatric symptoms.
- To investigate whether hospital staff can tell the sane from the insane.
- To test the **reliability** of a diagnosis of mental illness.

Where does it all go wrong?

Students mistakenly think that the pseudopatients are the participants – they're confederates.

Students focus on the first study only and forget about the contrasting second study where caution was reversed.

Procedure

Study 1

1   Rosenhan arranged for eight pseudopatients of various ages and occupations to present themselves to 12 different US psychiatric hospitals. None of the pseudopatients had a history of mental illness.
2   On arrival they each reported hearing voices including the words 'empty', 'hollow' and 'thud'. Beyond this, each stated the true facts of their lives but did not give their real name, occupation or reason for being there.
3   Once admitted to the psychiatric ward, the pseudopatients ceased simulating any symptoms of abnormality. The pseudopatients were told to behave 'normally'.
4   The pseudopatients were instructed to make notes about their environment. Initially this was done secretly, but it was soon clear that no one cared so it was done openly. The pseudopatients did not take their medications.
5   One of the conditions of taking part in the study was that they had to get out by their own devices.

Study 2

6   The staff at one of the hospitals were informed that at some time in the next three months, one or more pseudopatients would attempt to be admitted (none were).
7   Each member of staff was asked to rate all patients who sought admission using a 10-point scale; 1 and 2 reflected high confidence that the patient was a pseudopatient.

Study 3

8   One participant (either a pseudopatient or a young lady) approached a staff member (at a psychiatric hospital or on a college campus) and asked questions, as normally as possible, e.g. *Pardon me, Mr/Mrs/Dr X, could you tell me when I will be eligible for grounds privileges?*

Sample

The sample consisted of those individuals whose behaviour was being observed/measured. Therefore the pseudopatients were not the participants; they were **confederates**.

Study 1: The participants were the staff and real patients in 12 American mental hospitals. The hospitals represented a range of different kinds of psychiatric institutions – modern and old, well staffed and poorly staffed. Only one was private. This was an **opportunity sample**.

Study 2: Conducted in one hospital. The sample in this study was the staff of this hospital, including psychiatrists, psychologists and nurses.

Study 3: Involved staff at four of the mental hospitals and staff on a college campus.

(+) The sample of hospitals in the first part of the study represented a good range of psychiatric institutions, making the findings generalisable to US psychiatric hospitals.
(–) Only US hospitals were studied, therefore the findings may not apply in other cultures.

Research method/technique

The main two studies are **controlled observations**.

Null hypothesis = Psychiatric staff cannot distinguish sane from insane patients.

The third study is a **field experiment**.

IV = Pseudopatient or not

DV = Time spent responding

Hypothesis = Pseudopatients are spoken to for less time and given less complex answers than non-patients.

(+) The use of covert observation allowed the researchers to record how patients are treated/mistreated in many American psychiatric hospitals.
(–) The hospital staff may object to being observed without their consent.

Findings

Study 1
- Seven pseudopatients were diagnosed as **schizophrenic**.
- The nurses thought the writing behaviour of the pseudopatients was a sign of mental disorder.
- The staff treated the patients with little respect: punishing them for small incidents, beating them and swearing at them. Such treatment is **depersonalising** and creates an overwhelming sense of powerlessness.
- The average stay was 19 days (range 7–52 days).
- They were discharged with a diagnosis of 'schizophrenia in remission'.
- It may be that psychiatrists are more inclined to call a healthy person sick rather than calling a sick person healthy. It is more dangerous to misdiagnose someone as mentally ill as the label is 'sticky'.

Study 2
- 41 patients were judged with 'high confidence' to be pseudopatients by at least one staff member.
- 23 were suspected by at least one psychiatrist, 19 were suspected by a psychiatrist and one other staff member.
- Psychiatric staff compensated for previous results by being more inclined to call a sick person healthy.

Study 3
- Response to pseudopatients – 4% of the psychiatrists and 0.5% of the nurses stopped.
- Response to 'normal' young lady – all of the staff members stopped and answered all questions.

Quantitative data e.g. numbers of patients diagnosed as schizophrenic.

(+) Provides a simple measure of the effect of situational factors on diagnosis.
(–) Oversimplifies the complex system of diagnosis.

Qualitative data e.g. observations made by pseudopatients.

(+) Allows the researcher to gather rich, in-depth information about how staff interacted with and treated their patients.
(–) Such data is unique, making it difficult to analyse.

Describe how the individual differences approach could explain abnormality

The individual differences approach explains behaviour In terms of how people differ from each other rather than trying to just make generalisations about how people behave. Therefore it could explain abnormality because it focuses on how we distinguish between people who are abnormal or not abnormal (insane and sane).

Rosenhan showed that people were not diagnosed as abnormal on the basis of specific symptoms. Instead it was the situation (situational rather than dispositional explanation) that seemed to lead to a diagnosis. This suggests that it is actually very difficult to determine the difference between normality and abnormality and that psychiatric diagnosis is highly unreliable.

Section A type questions

In Section A of the G542 exam there will always be one question worth 4 marks on the study by Rosenhan (sane in insane places).

The questions below give you a taste of the kinds of questions you will be expected to answer on this section of the exam. In the exam each question would specifically mention Rosenhan (sane in insane places).

1   In the first part of this study pseudopatients sought to be admitted to various mental hospitals.
    (a)   Describe what the pseudopatients did to get themselves admitted to a psychiatric hospital. **[2]**
    (b)   Suggest **one** reason why doctors admitted the pseudopatients to hospital. **[2]**

2   Explain what happened in the second part of the study. **[4]**

3   In the first part of the study Rosenhan demonstrated that doctors preferred to make a mistake in the direction of caution, diagnosing a sane person as insane.
    (a)   Give **one** piece of evidence to support this. **[2]**
    (b)   Explain why it is more dangerous to make this mistake with mental illness than with physical illness. **[2]**

4   (a)   Give **one** example of how the pseudopatients' requests were dealt with by the staff. **[2]**
    (b)   Explain the reactions of the real patients to the pseudopatients. **[2]**

5   Rosenhan believed that the situation determined a diagnosis of abnormality rather than any individual factors. Outline **one** piece of evidence from the study that supports Rosenhan's view. **[4]**

6   'Once a person is designated abnormal, all of his other behaviours and characteristics are coloured by that label.' Describe **two** pieces of evidence from this study that support this statement. **[4]**

7   (a)   Identify **two** things the pseudopatients did which were labelled as abnormal by hospital staff. **[2]**
    (b)   Outline why these behaviours were labelled as abnormal. **[2]**

8   Rosenhan also conducted a mini-experiment where pseudopatients stopped staff members.
    (a)   Give an example of the question asked to a staff member. **[2]**
    (b)   Describe the typical response received by a pseudopatient. **[2]**

9   (a)   Describe **two** characteristics of the pseudopatients. **[2]**
    (b)   What instructions were the pseudopatients given to follow once they were admitted to hospital? **[2]**

10 Rosenhan suggested mental patients experienced powerlessness and depersonalisation.
    (a)   Outline **one** example that supports this suggestion. **[2]**
    (b)   Outline **one** possible explanation for the way hospital staff behaved towards the patients in this study. **[2]**

11 In the second study the staff at one of the hospitals were informed that at some time in the next three months, one or more pseudopatients would attempt to be admitted.
    (a)   How were their reactions recorded? **[2]**
    (b)   Give **one** conclusion that was drawn from this part of the study. **[2]**

12 Describe **two** ethical issues raised by Rosenhan's study 'On being sane in insane places'. **[4]**

13 (a)   What behaviours led the real patients to suspect that the pseudopatients were not real? **[2]**
    (b)   What was the average length of stay in hospital for a pseudopatient? **[2]**

14 (a)   Outline **one** way in which the sample may be considered representative. **[2]**
    (b)   Outline **one** way in which the sample may be considered unrepresentative. **[2]**

15 The pseudopatients in this study were not released from hospital for some time. Explain why it took so long for them to be discharged. **[4]**

16 Outline **two** ways in which this study can be said to be high in ecological validity. **[4]**

17 Rosenhan suggested the psychodiagnostic labels are 'sticky'.
    (a)   Give **one** piece of evidence to support this conclusion. **[2]**
    (b)   Describe **one** other conclusion that can be drawn from this study. **[2]**

18 (a)   Outline **two** ways that the pseudopatients' behaviour was standardised. **[2]**
    (b)   Explain why it is important that their behaviour was standardised. **[2]**

19 Outline **two** of the quantitative measures recorded in this study. **[4]**

20 When released, the pseudopatients were given the label 'schizophrenia in remission'.
    (a)   Explain the meaning of this label. **[2]**
    (b)   Give **one** conclusion that can be drawn from this. **[2]**

See www.psypress.com/
books/details/9781848721807/
for suggested answers.

Section B type questions

In Section B of the G542 exam you will be asked to provide detailed information about one core study. The questions will be similar to those below. You should practise answering these questions in relation to the study by Rosenhan (sane in insane places).

Background and aims

1 Outline previous research related to the study by Rosenhan. **[3]**

2 What was the aim of the study by Rosenhan? **[2]**

Design and procedure

3 Briefly outline the research method in this study. **[2]**

4 Explain why this study can be considered to be a covert observation. **[4]**

5 Suggest **one** strength of using this method in the context of this study. **[3]**

6 Suggest **one** weakness of using this method in the context of this study. **[3]**

7 Describe the sample used in this study. **[3]**

8 Explain how the sample in this study was selected. **[3]**

9 Suggest **one** strength of using this sample. **[3]**

10 Suggest **one** weakness of using this sample. **[3]**

11 Describe **two** ethical issues raised by this study. **[6]**

12 Outline the procedure followed by this study. **[8]**

13 Describe improvements/changes that could be made to this study. **[8]**

14 Evaluate the improvements/changes that you have suggested. **[8]**

Findings

15 Give **two** examples of quantitative data that was collected in this study. **[4]**

16 Suggest **one** strength of the quantitative data collected. **[3]**

17 Suggest **one** weakness of the quantitative data collected. **[3]**

18 Give **two** examples of qualitative data that was collected in this study. **[4]**

19 Suggest **one** strength of the qualitative data collected. **[3]**

20 Suggest **one** weakness of the qualitative data collected. **[3]**

21 Outline the findings of this study. **[8]**

22 Discuss the reliability of the findings of this study. **[6]**

23 Discuss the validity of the conclusions of this study. **[6]**

24 Discuss the ecological validity of this study. **[6]**

> **Example answer for question 3**
>
> *Sometimes a question is asked generally about the method used in a study, as here. In some studies there is clearly one method but in Rosenhan's study you could choose any one of the methods – covert observation, self-report or field experiment.*

> **Example answer for question 13**
>
> *Here is part of a possible answer:*
>
> *One change (if the study were done today) could be to use CCTV on the wards as well as the pseudopatients to collect data. This would mean that the pseudopatients would not have to take notes so much (and might not be thought of as so obsessive); and more data could be collected, even when the pseudopatient wasn't present*

> **Exam advice for question 19**
>
> *On page 69 one weakness of using quantitative data in this study is identified. Just stating this weakness would not be sufficient for 3 marks. You must always elaborate your answer so context and detail are included, as described on page 17.*

> **Exam advice for questions 23 and 24**
>
> *There is an overlap between these two questions because you could include material on ecological validity in an answer to question 23.*

Section C type questions

In Section C of the G542 exam there is one question (four parts) on the approaches/perspectives.

1 Outline **one** assumption of the individual differences approach. **[2]**

2 Describe how the individual differences approach could explain abnormality. **[4]**

3 Describe **one** similarity and **one** difference between the study by Rosenhan and any other study that has followed the individual differences approach. **[6]**

4 Discuss strengths and weaknesses of the individual differences approach using examples from the Rosenhan study. **[12]**

Thigpen and Cleckley

Aim

The aim of this study is to document the psychotherapeutic treatment of a 25-year-old woman who presented with a history of severe headaches and blackouts but was later discovered to have multiple personality disorder.

Context

Multiple personality disorder

Multiple personality disorder (MPD) is a psychiatric condition characterised by the occurrence of two or more personalities within the same individual, each of which is able to take control at some time in the person's life. Each personality is called an 'alter'. The 'alters' are said to occur spontaneously and involuntarily, and function more or less independently of each other. In the USA the condition is referred to as *Dissociative Identity Disorder (DID)*.

In the popular imagination MPD is commonly confused with **schizophrenia** because of the split personality aspect of it.

Research

MPD was reasonably well known in the 1950s, based on a few detailed **case histories** of patients exhibiting two or more people in one body.

However, such cases were rarely encountered by therapists and therefore the condition of MPD was viewed with some suspicion by psychiatrists.

The film The Three Faces of Eve *staring Joanne Woodward (who won an Oscar for her performance of Eve) was based on a book of the same name by Thigpen and Cleckley; both were released in 1957.*

Where does it all go wrong?

Students get confused between the psychometric tests and the projective tests – both measure psychological traits.

- **Psychometric tests** (e.g. IQ tests) produce quantitative data. The term literally means psychological measurement.
- **Projective tests** (e.g. ink blot tests) produce qualitative data. They assess personality by letting an individual respond freely, thus revealing unconscious thoughts and feelings.

Procedure

Collecting qualitative data

1   **Interviews** with Eve White (EW)/Eve Black (EB) – the main method used to collect information in this case study was the interviews between the two psychiatrists and EW/EB. Dr Thigpen and later Dr Cleckley spent 14 months (approximately 100 hours) interviewing EW/EB, collecting material about their thoughts, feelings and experiences. Initially, in order to interview EB, EW had to be hypnotised. Soon it became possible to simply ask to speak to EB and she would come forward.

2   Interviews with the patient's husband and family. The psychiatrists also talked to Eve's family to confirm some of the events she reported, such as being punished for wrongdoing that EB now claimed to be responsible for.

3   **Observations** by the psychiatrists of EW/EB's behaviour and facial expressions, such as observations of EB's provocative posture or EW's soft voice.

4   Interpretations by the psychiatrists of what the patient(s) reported, such as their view that Jane was a product genuinely different from both EW and EB.

5   Analysis of handwriting by a handwriting expert to determine whether EW and EB had different personalities.

6   Projective personality tests including the *Drawings of human figures test* and the *Rorschach ink blot test*. These were used to assess the different personalities of EW and EB.

Collecting quantitative data

7   **Psychometric tests**: IQ tests and memory tests were used to assess the differences between EW and EB.

8   **EEG** (encephalogram) was used to assess the **brain waves** of EW and EB as an objective measure of any physiological differences.

Sample

The sample was one person with three alters:

- 'Eve White' (EW) was referred to Dr Thigpen because she experienced severe headaches and blackouts.
- After several months of treatment a new 'person' emerged – Eve Black (EB), a very different personality. EB was aware of all EW did but the same was not true in reverse.
- A third personality, Jane, emerged during therapy. She was superficially a compromise between EW and EB.

(+) The appearance of an individual with a multiple personality allows psychiatrists to study the illness in depth, gaining new insights.
(–) Eve White's illness was 'unique' so one cannot generalise any findings to others who suffer MPD/DID.

Research method/technique

This is a **case study**, using **self-report** and **observation**.

(+) Because only one person was studied in depth a tremendous amount of detail could be gathered about the three different personalities, supported with evidence from the study.
(–) The researchers may have became emotionally involved with their participant and therefore lacked objectivity in the way they interpreted her behaviour.

Quantitative data e.g. scores on IQ test.

(+) Provides objective and simple way to make comparisons between the patients.
(–) Oversimplifies differences that may exist.

Qualitative data e.g. conversations with the patients.

(+) Rich, in-depth data provides insights into the factors that created the mental disorder.
(–) Difficult to analyse a complex record and draw simple conclusions.

Findings

Interviews and observations

- EW: Demure, face often looked sad, lacking boldness and spontaneity, industrious worker, devoted mother.
- EB: Party girl, childishly vain, immediately amusing and likeable, coarse voice, used slang, never hypnotised.
- Jane: superficially a compromise between EW and EB.
- Family members confirmed past events reported by EW and EB, e.g. being punished for wandering off through the woods to play with some other children, spending money on expensive clothes.

Qualitative and quantitative tests

- Handwriting expert: even though the handwritings superficially appeared to be by a different person, they all were clearly written by the same individual.
- Projective personality tests: EW was rigid and had difficulty dealing with her hostility (a **repressed** personality). EB had a healthier profile though she wished to return to an earlier period of life (a sign of **regression**).
- IQ test: EW scored 110 and EB scored 104.
- EEG: Tenseness was most pronounced in EB, next EW and then Jane. EW and Jane had a fairly similar **alpha rhythm** whereas EB's was a little bit faster, on the borderline between normal and abnormally fast.

Interpretations

- EW and EB might be seen as one personality at two stages of life.
- EB's role was to embody all the angry feelings, thus enabling EW to maintain a nice, loving persona.
- The therapists recognised that it would be morally wrong for them to 'kill off' any one personality.

Describe how the individual differences approach could explain MPD

The individual differences approach explains <u>behaviour</u> in terms of how people differ from each other rather than trying to just make generalisations about how people behave. Therefore it could explain MPD as a characteristic that is present in some people and not others.

Thigpen and Cleckley demonstrated this as a distinct disorder in the case that they studied.

Describe how the psychodynamic perspective could explain MPD

The psychodynamic perspective explains <u>behaviour</u> in terms of unconscious thoughts and feelings. Therefore it would explain MPD as an outcome of unconscious processes.

Eve White was not conscious of the presence of Eve Black who exerted pressure over how she behaved. It seems possible that the disorder developed because Eve repressed childhood anxieties as a method of dealing with feelings of hostility. Eve Black also exhibited signs of **ego defences** in her regression to more childlike behaviour, as a means of dealing with anxiety.

Section A type questions

In Section A of the G542 exam there will always be one question worth 4 marks on the study by Thigpen and Cleckley (multiple personality disorder).

The questions below give you a taste of the kinds of questions you will be expected to answer on this section of the exam. In the exam each question would specifically mention Thigpen and Cleckley (multiple personality disorder).

1   (a)   Outline the reasons why Eve first sought help from the psychiatrists. **[2]**
    (b)   Outline the real cause of her problems. **[2]**

2   Eve White was the main personality in this study. Describe the other **two** personalities. **[4]**

3   Thigpen and Cleckley used a number of different methods to gather data, including self-report.
    (a)   Describe **one** limitation of using the self-report method to gather data in this study. **[2]**
    (b)   Identify **two** other methods used in this study. **[2]**

4   (a)   Eve White was described as a 'repressed' personality. Explain what this means. **[2]**
    (b)   Explain what information she was repressing. **[2]**

5   An electroencephalograph (EEG) was used to measure an aspect of her behaviour.
    (a)   Explain what this measures. **[2]**
    (b)   Give the findings from using this measure. **[2]**

6   Explain the effect of Eve Black on Eve White's thoughts and behaviour. **[4]**

7   Eve Black was described as a 'regressed' personality.
    (a)   Explain how the psychiatrists tested her personality. **[2]**
    (b)   Explain what a 'regressed personality' is. **[2]**

8   (a)   Identify **two** psychometric tests carried out on the patients in this study. **[2]**
    (b)   Outline the findings of **one** of these tests. **[2]**

9   Projective personality tests were used in this study.
    (a)   Explain how such tests measure personality. **[2]**
    (b)   Outline the findings of **one** of these tests. **[2]**

10   Outline **two** limitations of the findings of this study. **[4]**

11   (a)   Give **one** reason why the data in this study may not be considered to be reliable. **[2]**
     (b)   Give **one** reason why the data in this study may not be considered to be valid. **[2]**

12   Describe **two** pieces of evidence that could support the claim that the patient did have multiple personality disorder (MPD). **[4]**

13   (a)   Describe an event that the patient recalled from earlier in her life. **[2]**
     (b)   Explain how this event provided insight into this case study. **[2]**

14   Outline **two** ethical problems that may arise when psychologists study people with mental disorders. **[2]**

15   Describe **one** of the personalities in this study. **[4]**

16   Family members were also interviewed by Thigpen and Cleckley.
     (a)   Give **one** example of information provided by a relative of the patient. **[2]**
     (b)   Explain the importance of this information in understanding this case. **[2]**

17   Thigpen and Cleckley acknowledged that they may have played a role in 'creating' Jane. Describe their views of this third personality. **[4]**

18   (a)   Give **one** piece of evidence that suggests the patient did not have multiple personality disorder. **[2]**
     (b)   Give **one** limitation of this piece of evidence. **[2]**

19   (a)   Outline **one** way in which the sample may be considered representative. **[2]**
     (b)   Outline **one** way in which the sample may be considered unrepresentative. **[2]**

20   (a)   What is a leading question? **[2]**
     (b)   How might leading questions affect the results of this study? **[2]**

See www.psypress.com/books/ details/9781848721807/ for suggested answers.

Section B type questions

In Section B of the G542 exam you will be asked to provide detailed information about one core study. The questions will be similar to those below. You should practise answering these questions in relation to the study by Thigpen and Cleckley (multiple personality disorder).

Background and aims

1   Outline previous research related to the study by Thigpen and Cleckley. [3]
2   What was the aim of the study by Thigpen and Cleckley? [2]

Design and procedure

3   Explain why this study can be considered to be a case study. [4]
4   Suggest **one** strength of using this method in the context of this study. [3]
5   Suggest **one** weakness of using this method in the context of this study. [3]
6   Describe the sample used in this study. [3]
7   Explain why this sample was chosen. [3]
8   Suggest **one** strength of using this sample. [3]
9   Suggest **one** weakness of using this sample. [3]
10 Explain why this study can be considered a longitudinal study. [4]
11 With reference to this study, suggest **one** strength of conducting longitudinal studies. [3]
12 With reference to this study, suggest **one** weakness of conducting longitudinal studies. [3]
13 Outline the procedure followed by this study. [8]
14 Describe improvements/changes that could be made to this study. [8]
15 Evaluate the improvements/changes that you have suggested. [8]

Example answer for question 7

Questions about samples include what or how or why. In this case the question is 'why' and the answer would be:

The patient Eve was selected because she had consulted the psychiatrists about her headaches and blackouts that had no physical cause. This gave Thigpen and Cleckley the opportunity to study her in depth and report on her experiences and thoughts.

Findings

16 Give **two** examples of quantitative data that was collected in this study. [4]
17 Suggest **one** strength of the quantitative data collected. [3]
18 Suggest **one** weakness of the quantitative data collected. [3]
19 Give **two** examples of qualitative data that was collected in this study. [4]
20 Suggest **one** strength of the qualitative data collected. [3]
21 Suggest **one** weakness of the qualitative data collected. [3]
22 Outline the findings of this study. [8]
23 Discuss the reliability of the findings of this study. [6]
24 Discuss the validity of the conclusions of this study. [6]
25 Discuss the ecological validity of this study. [6]

Exam advice for question 15

'Evaluate' often means give the strengths and/ or weaknesses – which is one way to approach this question. You can consider the strengths or you might consider the weaknesses of the suggestions you have made.

'Evaluate' also means 'assess', so you can also simply consider the consequences of your suggestions.

Exam advice for question 24

When considering the validity of the conclusions this could involve the effect of leading questions and/or the validity of the tests used.

Section C type questions

In Section C of the G542 exam there is one question (four parts) on the approaches/perspectives.

1   Outline **one** assumption of the individual differences approach. [2]
2   Describe how the individual differences approach could explain multiple personality disorder. [4]
3   Describe **one** similarity and **one** difference between the study by Thigpen and Cleckley and any other study that has followed the individual differences approach. [6]
4   Discuss strengths and weaknesses of the individual differences approach using examples from the Thigpen and Cleckley study. [12]

You should answer this question in relation to the psychodynamic perspective as well.

Aim

The aim of this study is to increase understanding of the cognitive processes and behaviour of persistent fruit machine gamblers.

Specifically the aim is to compare the cognitive processes of regular fruit machine gamblers (RGs) and non-regular fruit machine gamblers (NRGs) to see if RGs are more irrational.

Context

Heuristics

Psychologists have sought to understand gambling by looking at what people are thinking when they gamble. Thought processes can be described in terms of **heuristics** – strategies used to work something out or solve a problem. A heuristic may be a set of rules (such as a recipe for a cake), an educated guess or just common sense. It is a guideline of what to do in specific situations.

You may have some general heuristics for solving problems, such as *if it doesn't work try reading the instructions* or *if I want to know what's on TV tonight I check the listing in the newspaper* or *when my teacher asks a question I just say the first thing that pops into my head*. It's a plan of action.

Cognitive biases

Heuristics can present a distorted picture of the world and may lead to **cognitive biases**. For example, the *illusion of control* distorts reality because we erroneously believe we have control over events.

Where does it all go wrong?

There are a few difficult concepts:

* **Cognitive bias** – The word 'cognitive' means 'thinking'. The word 'bias' means 'leaning in one direction'. So cognitive bias is about the fact that we all tend to think in bent ways!
* **Analysis of thinking aloud** – Some students don't understand what is going on. Try the thinking aloud method yourself.

There are a lot of findings in this study so take time to tease them out. Use the headings on the facing page to help you structure the findings.

Procedure

The task

1   Each participant was given £3 to gamble on a fruit machine in a local arcade (this amount of money was equivalent to 30 free plays).
2   Participants were asked to play the game called 'FRUITSKILL' unless they objected – some players did choose a different game.
3   Participants were asked to try to stay on their machine for at least 60 gambles (i.e. they would break even and win back £3).
4   After the 60 gambles point they were allowed to either keep the £3 or carry on gambling.

Forms of assessment:

5   **Behavioural** – The skill of RGs and NRGs was observed on seven **dependent variables**: total plays, total time, play rate, end stake, wins, win rate (time) and win rate (plays).
6   **Thinking aloud** – Half the RGs and half the NRGs were asked to think aloud while playing to gain insight into their cognitive processes.
7   They were given **standardised instructions** advising them to say everything that went through their mind and to speak in complete sentences. These verbalisations were tape-recorded.
8   **Post-experiment** **semi-structured interview** – Participants were asked their opinion about the level of skill involved in fruit machine playing and asked to judge their own skill level.

Sample

Sixty participants took part: 30 regular gamblers (RGs) and 30 non-regular gamblers (NRGs), all from Devon, UK. RGs gambled at least once a week, NRGs gambled once a month or less (but had used fruit machines at least once).

There was a gender imbalance in the RG group (29 males and one female). The **mean** age was 23.4 years.

The NRG group consisted of 15 males and 15 females, mean age 25.3.

The participants were recruited through poster advertisements around local university and college campuses (**self-selected sample**). Some of the RGs were recruited via a gambler known to the researcher.

(+) Although there were 29 regular male gamblers but only one regular female gambler, this could be considered a representative sample because fruit machine gambling is very male-dominated. Results could therefore be generalised to the gambling population as a whole.

(–) All participants were from Devon, a rural area, so the findings may not be generalisable.

Research method/technique

This is a **quasi-experiment** as the IV varied naturally. It was conducted in the field. It used an **independent measures** design.

IV = RG or NRG

DV = Skill, verbalisations, speed

Hypotheses
- There are no differences between RGs and NRGs in terms of skill.
- RGs produce more irrational verbalisations when gambling than NRGs.
- RGs regard themselves as more skilled at fruit machine gambling than NRGs.
- Participants in the thinking aloud condition would take longer than 'non-thinking aloud' participants.

(+) Using **self-report** provides insight into the thought processes of the gamblers.

(–) Using someone else's money may reduce the excitement and risk taking involved in gambling.

Quantitative data e.g. total number of minutes played during one play session, number of irrational verbalisations.

(+) Allows identification of patterns of behaviour, can calculate averages, results easy to analyse.

(–) No explanation for why the behaviour occurred.

Qualitative data e.g. interviews with participants.

(+) Provides insight into the reasons for their behaviour.

(–) Difficult to analyse and draw simple conclusions about why people behaved as they did.

Findings

Behavioural data

The only two **significant** differences on the DVs were:
- RGs had a significantly higher playing rate (eight gambles per minute as compared to six per minute for NRGs).
- RGs who thought aloud had a significantly lower win rate in number of gambles (i.e. the number of gambles between each win was significantly lower than for NRGs).

A further, highly significant difference was:
- Ten of the 14 RGs who broke even after 60 gambles (71%) carried on gambling until they had lost everything, whereas only two out of the seven (29%) NRGs who broke even carried on.

Analysis of thinking aloud

- RGs produced significantly more irrational verbalisations (14%) than did NRGs (2.5%), e.g. **personification** of the machine.
- RGs referred to their mind going blank and feeling frustrated, topics rarely mentioned by NRGs.
- RGs in the thinking aloud group had the longest intervals between wins.

Analysis of interview

- Most NRGs said skill on fruit machines was *mostly chance*, whereas most RGs said *equal chance and skill*.
- NRGs viewed themselves as below average, whereas RGs said *above average* or *totally skilled*.

Describe how the individual differences approach could explain gambling addiction

The individual differences approach explains behaviour in terms of how people differ from each other rather than trying to just make generalisations about how people behave. Therefore it could explain gambling addiction in terms of why some people become gamblers whereas others don't.

Griffiths, in his study into fruit machine gambling, looked at the behaviours of regular and non-regular gamblers. He found regular gamblers were more likely than non-regular gamblers to personalise the machine by saying such things as *The machine likes me*, and to make more irrational vocalisations than non-regular gamblers such as *I lost because I wasn't concentrating*. Such behaviours show that regular gamblers behave differently to non-regular gamblers, supporting the view that individual differences are strong factors affecting gambling behaviour.

Section A type questions

In Section A of the G542 exam there will always be one question worth 4 marks on the study by Griffiths (gambling).

The questions below give you a taste of the kinds of questions you will be expected to answer on this section of the exam. In the exam each question would specifically mention Griffiths (gambling).

1 (a) Identify **two** dependent variables (DVs) in this experiment. **[2]**
   (b) Describe **one** effect the independent variable (IV) had on **one** of these dependent variables (DVs). **[2]**

2 (a) Outline why this study is considered to be an experiment. **[2]**
   (b) Explain why this study is not a field experiment. **[2]**

3 This study had four hypotheses.
   (a) State **one** of these hypotheses. **[2]**
   (b) Explain how the results of this study support **one** of its hypotheses. **[2]**

4 Explain how Griffiths used the 'quasi-experimental' method in his study into fruit machine gambling. **[4]**

5 (a) Identify the experimental design used in this study. **[2]**
   (b) Give **one** weakness in using this experimental design. **[2]**

6 In this study each participant was given £3 to gamble on a fruit machine.
   (a) Describe the gambling task each participant was then set. **[2]**
   (b) Explain why all participants were asked to use the same fruit machine. **[2]**

7 One of the dependent variables (DVs) in this study was the skill level of the players. This was assessed by interviewing them.
   (a) Describe **one** other method used to measure skill levels. **[2]**
   (b) Suggest **one** problem with assessing skill level in this way. **[2]**

8 Some of the findings are shown in the table below.

	Play rate (per minute)	% irrational verbalisations
Regular gamblers	8	14
Non-regular gamblers	6	2.5

   (a) Outline **one** conclusion that can be drawn from this table. **[2]**
   (b) Explain why it was necessary to have two groups of participants. **[2]**

9 Describe the procedure for the 'thinking aloud' condition in this study. **[4]**

10 (a) Outline **one** way in which the sample of gamblers may be considered representative. **[2]**
   (b) Outline **one** way in which the sample of gamblers may be considered unrepresentative. **[2]**

11 (a) Describe **one** similarity between the results of regular and non-regular gamblers. **[2]**
   (b) Describe **one** difference between the results of regular and non-regular gamblers. **[2]**

12 (a) Identify **two** criteria used to select the participants in this study. **[2]**
   (b) Explain why the researchers could not manipulate the independent variable (IV). **[2]**

13 Participants were interviewed about their skills levels.
   (a) Give **one** strength of using this method in this study. **[2]**
   (b) Give **one** weakness of using this method in this study. **[2]**

14 Outline **two** ways in which this study could be considered ethical. **[4]**

15 Outline **one** piece of evidence from the study that supports the view that gamblers experience cognitive bias (distortion of thinking). **[4]**

16 Outline **two** ways in which this study can be said to be high in ecological validity. **[4]**

17 (a) Give **one** example of an irrational verbalisation. **[2]**
   (b) Give **one** conclusion that was drawn related to irrational verbalisations. **[2]**

18 (a) Outline how the thinking aloud task was standardised. **[2]**
   (b) Aside from thinking aloud task, outline **one** other task used in the study. **[2]**

19 (a) Give **one** reason why the data may not be considered to be reliable. **[2]**
   (b) Give **one** reason why the data may not be considered to be valid. **[2]**

20 (a) Identify **two** controls used in this study. **[2]**
   (b) Explain why **one** of these controls was used. **[2]**

See www.psypress.com/books/details/9781848721807/ for suggested answers.

Section B type questions

In Section B of the G542 exam you will be asked to provide detailed information about one core study. The questions will be similar to those below. You should practise answering these questions in relation to the study by Griffiths (gambling).

Background and aims

1 Outline previous research related to the study by Griffiths. **[3]**
2 What was the aim of the study by Griffiths? **[2]**
3 State **one** hypothesis investigated in this study. **[2]**

Design and procedure

4 Explain why this study can be considered to be a quasi-experiment. **[4]**
5 Suggest **one** strength of using this method in the context of this study. **[3]**
6 Suggest **one** weakness of using this method in the context of this study. **[3]**
7 Describe the sample used in this study. **[3]**
8 Explain how the sample in this study was selected. **[3]**
9 Suggest **one** strength of using this sample. **[3]**
10 Suggest **one** weakness of using this sample. **[3]**
11 Describe **two** ethical issues raised by this study. **[6]**
12 Outline the procedure followed by this study. **[8]**
13 Describe improvements/changes that could be made to this study. **[8]**
14 Evaluate the improvements/changes that you have suggested. **[8]**

Findings

15 Give **two** examples of quantitative data that was collected in this study. **[4]**
16 Suggest **one** strength of the quantitative data collected. **[3]**
17 Suggest **one** weakness of the quantitative data collected. **[3]**
18 Give **two** examples of qualitative data that was collected in this study. **[4]**
19 Suggest **one** strength of the qualitative data collected. **[3]**
20 Suggest **one** weakness of the qualitative data collected. **[3]**
21 Outline the findings of this study. **[8]**
22 Discuss the reliability of the findings of this study. **[6]**
23 Discuss the validity of the conclusions of this study. **[6]**
24 Discuss the ecological validity of this study. **[6]**

Exam advice

Throughout the core study part of this book there are many different pieces of exam advice – review them all to check that you remember how to maximise your marks.

Example answer for question 16

On the previous spread both strengths and weaknesses are described very briefly. For a three mark answer you need to be able to expand the content. For example:

One strength of quantitative data is that it allows identification of patterns of behaviour and results are easy to analyse.

LINK TO STUDY...

In the study by Griffiths he counted the number of utterances made by gamblers and non-regular gamblers. Then he could see patterns in the behaviour of the participants, for example he looked at the different kinds of utterances (rational and irrational). Then he could analyse this and easily draw conclusions about the cognitive biases of gamblers.

Section C type questions

In Section C of the G542 exam there is one question (four parts) on the approaches/perspectives.

1 Outline **one** assumption of the individual differences approach. **[2]**
2 Describe how the individual differences approach could explain gambling. **[4]**
3 Describe **one** similarity and **one** difference between the study by Griffiths and any other study that has followed the individual differences approach. **[6]**
4 Discuss strengths and weaknesses of the individual differences approach using examples from the Griffiths study. **[12]**

Exam advice on question 3

There are three marks for each – so you must make sure you provide sufficient detail.

A

abnormal A psychological condition or behaviour that departs from the norm or is harmful and distressing to the individual or those around them. Abnormal behaviours are usually those that violate society's ideas of what is an appropriate level of functioning. 68, 69, 73

alpha rhythm A brain wave characteristic of the brain when it is relaxed, the waves are more regular than when awake and have a greater amplitude (i.e. the height of the wave is larger). 73

alternate hypothesis A testable statement about the relationship between two variables. Alternative to the null hypothesis. 12, 14

anonymity Not being identifiable; a means of dealing with the ethical issue of privacy. 4

Asperger syndrome An autistic spectrum disorder where individuals are deficient in social skills but, unlike other autistics, have a normal IQ. Some individuals (although not all) exhibit exceptional skill or talent in a specific area. 24

attrition The loss of participants from a study over time, which is likely to leave a biased sample or a sample that is too small for reliable analysis. 5, 18

authoritarianism Favouring absolute obedience to authority, either by submitting to authority or wielding authority. 60, 61

autism A mental disorder which usually appears in early childhood and typically involves avoidance of social contact, abnormal language, and so-called 'stereotypic' or bizarre behaviours. 24, 25

autistic spectrum disorder (ASD) A classification that unites a range of different disorders that share similar characteristics, such as difficulty in social relationships and difficulty in understanding what is in other people's minds. 'Low' functioning autism is at one end of the spectrum and 'high' functioning Asperger syndrome at the other end. 24

B

bar chart A graph used to represent the frequency of data. The categories on the x-axis have no fixed order, and there is no true zero. 6

behaviour checklist An operationalised list of the behaviours to be recorded during an observational study. 8

behavioural categories Operationalising a target behaviour, i.e. dividing it into a set of constituent behaviours. These can be used in the form of a behaviour checklist or a coding system. 8, 9, 36

behaviourist The view that all behaviour can be explained as a result of classical or operant conditioning (i.e. nurture, environment). The approach is only concerned with the behaviours themselves rather than any internal mechanisms – thus 'behaviourism'. 19

brain wave The brain produces electrical signals that vary in voltage. A brain wave is the rapid alternation between high and low voltage. This voltage change is translated by an EEG machine into a series of wavy lines. 48, 72

bystander behaviour The presence of others (bystanders) reduces the likelihood that help will be offered in an emergency situation. 64

C

case study A research method that involves a detailed study of a single individual, institution or event. Case studies provide a rich record of human experience but are hard to generalise from. 18, 19, 29, 40, 41, 49, 53, 61, 72, 73

ceiling effect An effect that occurs when test items are too easy for a group of individuals. Therefore too many people do very well, i.e. 'hit the ceiling'. 25

classical conditioning Learning that occurs through association. A neutral stimulus is paired with an unconditioned stimulus, resulting in a new stimulus–response (S–R) link. 19, 36, 57

closed question A question that has a range of answers from which respondents select one; produces quantitative data. Answers are easier to analyse than those for open questions. 10

co-variable The measured variables in a correlational analysis. The variables must be continuous. 14

coding system A systematic method for recording observations in which individual behaviours are given a code for ease of recording. 8

cognitive alternatives 'Cognitive' refers to the process of thinking (knowing, perceiving, believing), so cognitive alternatives are giving a person different ways to think about a situation. 60, 61

cognitive bias A distortion of judgement or thinking that occurs in particular situations. 76

cohort effect An effect caused because one group of participants has unique characteristics due to time-specific experiences during their development. 18

confederate An individual in an experiment who is not a real participant and has been instructed how to behave by the investigator. 57, 65, 68, 69

confidentiality An ethical issue concerned with a participant's right to have personal information protected. 4, 10

conservation The ability to distinguish between reality and appearance, for example to understand that quantity is not changed even when a display is transformed. 32, 33

control condition In an experiment with a repeated measures design, the condition that provides a baseline measure of behaviour without the experimental treatment, so that the effect of the experimental treatment may be assessed. 12

control group In an experiment with an independent groups design, a group of participants who receive no treatment. Their behaviour acts as a baseline against which the effect of the independent variable may be measured. 12, 20, 25, 36, 45

controlled observation A form of investigation in which behaviour is observed but under conditions where certain variables have been organised by the researcher. 8, 49, 53, 57, 61, 69

G

grey matter The term used to describe certain parts of the brain. It is found on the surface of the brain and also deep inside, in structures such as the hypothalamus and hippocampus. It is the part of the brain that is most dense in neural connections (which makes it look grey) and is associated with higher order thinking. **44**

H

helping behaviour Providing assistance for someone in need. **64, 65**

hemisphere (brain) The forebrain is divided into two halves or hemispheres. Each half is largely the same, containing the same specialised regions with the exception of those functions that are lateralised, such as language. **44, 52, 53**

hemisphere deconnection *see* **split-brain**

heuristic A strategy used to solve a problem or work something out. It can be a set of rules, an educated guess or just common sense. **76**

hippocampus A structure in the subcortical area of each hemisphere of the forebrain (i.e. 'under' the cortex, deep inside the brain). It is associated with memory. It is part of the limbic system, therefore involved in motivation, emotion and learning. **44, 45**

hypothesis A precise and testable statement about the world, specifically of the relationship between data to be measured. It is a statement about populations and not samples. **12, 17**

I

independent measures An experimental design in which participants are allocated to two (or more) groups representing different research conditions. Allocation is achieved using random or systematic techniques. **12, 21, 25, 33, 37, 45, 65, 77**

independent variable (IV) In an experiment, an event that is directly manipulated by an experimenter in order to test its effect on another variable (the dependent variable). **12, 57**

informed consent An ethical issue and an ethical guideline in psychological research whereby participants are given comprehensive information concerning the nature and purpose of the research and their role in it, in order that they can make an informed decision about whether to participate. **4, 8**

inter-rater reliability The extent to which there is agreement between two or more observers (raters). **8**

intervening variable A variable that comes between two other variables and can be used to explain the relationship between the two variables. **14**

interview A research method that involves a face-to-face, 'real-time' interaction with another individual and results in the collection of data. **4, 10, 52, 72, 76**

interviewer bias The effect of an interviewer's expectations, communicated unconsciously, on a respondent's behaviour. **10**

IQ test A test of mental ability based on a theoretical view of what intelligence is. **73**

IV *see* **independent variable**

laboratory Any setting (a room or other environment) specially fitted out for conducting research. **8, 19, 48, 56, 57, 64**

L

laboratory experiment An experiment carried out in the controlled setting of a laboratory. **12, 21, 33, 37, 65**

lateralised Brain functions that are largely controlled by one side of the brain, such as language which is governed by the left hemisphere. **52**

leading question A question that is phrased in such a way that it makes one response more likely than another (e.g. 'Don't you agree that...?') **10, 20, 21, 41**

legitimacy The extent to which something is fair or right. **56, 57, 60, 61**

lexigram A symbol used to represent a word but not necessarily indicative of the object referenced by the word. **28, 29**

longitudinal A study conducted over a long period of time. Often a form of repeated measures design in which participants are assessed on two or more occasions as they get older. **18, 21, 29, 41**

M

matched Making two or more groups of participants similar with respect to key characteristics such as age, essentially a matched participants design. **25, 45, 60**

matched pairs design An experimental design in which pairs of participants are matched in terms of variables relevant to the study, such as age, IQ, perceptual ability and so on. One member of each pair receives one level of the IV and the second pair member receives the other level of the IV. This means that participant variables are better controlled than is usually the case in an independent groups design experiment. **37**

mean A measure of central tendency. The arithmetic average of a group of scores, calculated by dividing the sum of the scores by the number of scores. **6, 21, 25, 33, 37, 45, 65, 77**

median A measure of central tendency. The middle value in a set of scores when they are placed in rank order. **6, 65**

modal group The group that has the most common scores/items. **6**

mode A measure of central tendency. The most frequently occurring score in a set of data. **6**

model A person who is imitated. **36, 37, 65, 66**

MRI scan Magnetic resonance imaging, produces a three-dimensional image of the static, living brain which is very precise and provides information about the function of different regions of the brain. It is also used to scan other parts of the body. **44**

multiple personality disorder A type of mental disorder where two or more relatively independent personalities are believed to exist in one person. The separate personalities have become 'dissociated' (separated) from each other, thus the name 'dissociative personality disorder' is also used. Dissociation may occur as a consequence of stress. 72, 73

N

naturalistic observation A research method carried out in a naturalistic setting, in which the investigator does not interfere in any way but merely observes the behaviour(s) in question. 8

nature Those aspects of behaviour that are innate and inherited. 'Nature' does not simply refer to abilities present at birth but to any ability determined by genes, including those that appear throughout the lifespan through maturation, such as changes at puberty. 19

negative correlation A relationship between two co-variables such that as the value of one co-variable increases, that of the other decreases. 14, 45

NREM sleep Non-rapid eye movement sleep; sleep during which there are no random eye movements (i.e. all the other parts of sleep excepting when there is REM!). 48, 49

null hypothesis An assumption that there is no relationship (difference, association, etc.) in the population from which a sample is taken with respect to the variables being studied. 14, 14, 69

nurture Those aspects of behaviour that are acquired through experience, i.e. learned from interactions with the physical and social environment. 19

O

obedience A type of social influence whereby somebody acts in response to a direct order from a figure with perceived authority. There is also the implication that the person receiving the order is made to respond in a way that they would not otherwise have done without the order. 56, 57

observation/observational study A research technique where a researcher watches or listens to participants engaging in whatever behaviour is being studied. 4, 8, 14, 28, 36, 39, 49, 53, 57, 61, 63, 69, 72, 73

observational learning Another term for social learning; learning by observing others. 37

observational techniques The application of systematic strategies to record observation data, such as the use of time sampling or behavioural categories. 8, 37, 65

observer bias In observational studies, the danger that observers' expectations affect what they see or hear. 8

Oedipus complex Freud's explanation of how a boy resolves his love for his mother and feelings of rivalry towards his father by identifying with his father. Occurs during the phallic stage of psychosexual development. 40, 42

one-tailed hypothesis States the direction of difference (e.g. more or less) between two groups of participants or between different conditions, or the relationship (positive or negative) between co-variables. 14

one-way mirror A mirror that is reflective on one side but transparent on the other. This allows observers to watch participants without them being aware of the observers' presence (covert observation). 36

open question In an interview or questionnaire, a question that invites respondents to provide their own answers rather than select one of those provided. Tends to produce qualitative data. 10

operant conditioning Learning that occurs when we are reinforced for doing something, which increases the probability that the behaviour in question will be repeated in the future. Conversely, if we are punished for behaving in a certain way, there is a decrease in the probability that the behaviour will recur. 19, 36, 57

operationalise Providing variables in a form that can be easily tested. 12, 19

opportunity sample A sample of participants produced by selecting people who are most easily available at the time of the study. 5, 29, 33, 37, 41, 45, 49, 69

order effect In a repeated measures design, an extraneous variable arising from the order in which conditions are presented. 12

P

participant observation Observations made by someone who is also participating in the activity being observed, which may affect their objectivity. 8

participant variable Characteristics of individual participants (such as age, intelligence, etc.) that might influence the outcome of a study. 12, 18, 33

permeability Refers to the ability to move from one place to another. A membrane that is permeable allows substances to pass through it. 60, 61

personification Attributing human characteristics to animals, inanimate objects, or abstract notions. 77

phallic stage In psychoanalytic theory, the third stage of psychosexual development when the organ-focus is on the genitals. Resolution of this stage results in the development of a superego. 40, 41

phobia A group of mental disorders characterised by high levels of anxiety that, when experienced, interfere with normal living. 40, 41

pilot study A trial run of a research study, involving only a few participants who are representative of the target population. It is conducted to test any aspects of the research design, with a view to making improvements before conducting the full research study. 8, 56

positive correlation A relationship between two co-variables such that as the value of one co-variable increases, this is accompanied by a corresponding increase in the other co-variable. 14, 45, 49

presumptive consent A method of dealing with lack of informed consent or deception, by asking a group of people who are similar to the participants whether they would agree to take part in a study. If this group of people consent to the procedures in the proposed study, it is presumed that the real participants would agree as well. 4